INDIAN GIVER:

Warren Lowes

INDIAN GIVER

A Legacy of North American
Native Peoples

URBAN FIRST NATIONS EDUCATION CENTRE
THE LEARNING CENTRE
Suite 204 - 668 Carnarvon Street
New Westminster, B.C. V3M 5Y6

Warren Lowes

Copyright 1986: Canadian Alliance in
Solidarity with Native People. (CASNP)

                    Canadian Cataloging in Publication Data

Lowes, Warren, 1919-1983
Indian Giver

ISBN 0-919441-25-4

1. Canada-Civilization-Indian influences.
2. United States-Civilization-Indian influences.
I. Title.
E77.L68 1985 303.4'8271 C85-091090-0

Cover Art by Leland Bell
Cover Design by Beyond Graphics

Typeset by Theytus Books
Penticton, B.C.

Printed and Bound in Canada

'Warren Lowes' thoughts about the earth and the sun are correct in regard to Native conviction and they also correspond to the recovered insights of non-Natives. A physicist (Sr. Eva Bertell) said recently, "The earth is a living system, pulsing, balanced, recycling". A European scholar writes about the sun as "...the centre of the material world, it is also the great sign and symbol of that Heart which is the centre of all things".

In these matters Lowes' relates Native insights to matter that are of the utmost importance today and I found his writing gratifying indeed.'

Dr. Ed Newbery, Professor Emeritus,
Native Studies Department,
University of Sudbury, Ontario.

"When we consider the material conquests of the ancient Mayas in architecture, sculpture, ceramics, and on a smaller scale their work in carved stone and feathers, their weaving and cotton dyes; together with the intellectual progess in the field of the abstract—the invention of writing and of positional arithmetic, and their development of the concept of zero; the construction of the complicated calendar and a chronology that stemmed from a fixed starting point, both of them as exact as our Gregorian calendar; a knowledge of astronomy superior to that of the Egyptians and Babylonians, and we take time to analyze the product of their civilization in the light of their known cultural limitations, we can without fear of contradiction proclaim the Mayans as the most brilliant indigenous people on the planet."

Sylvanus Morley
Archaeologist

TABLE OF CONTENTS

ACKNOWLEDGEMENTS

Whatever contribution to scholarship this book may contain is in large measure the result of the labours and talents of persons other than the author. Such a work must, by its very nature, be the compilation from a multitude of sources—books, journals, magazines, and newspapers. In some specific cases, I have stated the source of the information. In addition, I would like to mention the writings of such authors as Dee Brown, Wilfred Pelletier, P.G. Poole, T.C. McLuhan, Gayle High Pine, and Stan Steiner. I would like to express thanks to the Staff and members of the Canadian Association in Support of Native Peoples for assistance and constructive advice, and I am grateful to my Ojibway friend, Wilber Ingersoll, for consultative assistance.

Publication was made possible with the generous assistance of Mildred Beggs and the estate of Lila Bacon.

Especially, I give thanks for the patience of my wife, Bjorg Lowes, whose help in typing and re-typing manuscript copy, was given without stint.

PREFACE

This is a book about people—a particular People. Its general concern is with relationships, and its particular interest centres upon the contributions which these People have made to the well-being of the larger human family. During the eons of time that man has inhabited the earth, he has wandered over its face as an inquisitive, searching creature. Geographic landscapes, changing from time to time through glacial movements, floods, earthquakes and continental drift, have caused some members to become isolated, and others to be thrown together.

This book does not presume to trace the wanderings of North America's Native Peoples, nor to dwell on incidents of inter-human conflict. Rather, it attempts, in a limited way, to scan the more recent years of history, and to show in very broad outline what these very remarkable people, isolated as they were from other branches of the human family, were able to accomplish.

It will further attempt to describe how these influences have now become so indelibly inscribed upon the lifestyle of the whole, that these effects can never be erased.

We apologize for the use of non-inclusive language ('man' in the sense of the 'human being'). If Native languages were used, this problem would not arise as their commonly used words for people are non-sexist. This problem illustrates the deeper problem of a foreign culture perceiving others only through the lens of its own value structure, and thus distorting, misunderstanding, and then destroying.

INTRODUCTION

Over the past four hundred years, in this hemisphere, there has been in progress one of the most significant social happenings of all time—the intermingling of people from various social backgrounds, the ethnic amalgamation of some, and a medley of confusion with others. It has been as though elements of unknown substances were thrown together in a laboratory, without consideration of their various properties, while a group of self-appointed observers stand aside trying to understand and explain what is going on. The principals who are involved are not substances—they are people—and the observers are variously described as ethnologists, anthropologists and social psychologists.

As we know, both the continents of North and South America had been populated for twelve thousand years or more—perhaps thirty thousand years. The aboriginal people, in some places thinly scattered and in others more compactly associated, had formed themselves into societies that ranged from roving tribes of a few families to the more involved social organizations known as confederations and city-states.

In Europe, we must not forget, a parallel situation had also prevailed. Various tribal groups had wandered across the face of Europe and Asia, sometimes plundering their neighbours and sometimes settling down to form nations. Some inquisitive elements of these societies had taken time to study out the secrets of physical science which permitted wider travel by land and water. Others, less adventurous, had devised methods to record information and dabbled in the art of organizing other people to do their bidding. It was an amalgamation of these two points of interest that produced the feudal state, and Europe was firmly in the grip of this particular form of despotism when adventurers such as Columbus, Cortes and Cartier arrived on the shores of the Americas.

These are simple statements of recorded history. But they are fundamental to an understanding of what has transpired in the past four hundred years.

In the initial stages, the flow of newcomers to the New World was a mere trickle. But as the riches of nature's bounty in North America became more evident, and the chances of escape from the clutches of the feudal lords became more inviting, the emigration grew into a flood. In the past two hundred years, immigrants have arrived in such waves that some experts now feel that the land base cannot support many more. In a sense, the end of an era is fast approaching.

But while this immigration has continued, each of the national groups— French, British, Spanish, German, Slav, Scandinavian and a long list of others—has brought along its own particular cultural characteristics. Some of them have much in common; others differ in lesser detail. But most were brought into close contact with the cultures of the Native Peoples whose outlook and methods differed vastly from all the newcomers because of the thousands of years they had lived separately from the rest of the human family.[1]

Here was a field of study for ethnologists and anthropologists that would set them thinking as never before. Who are these people? Where did they originate? What are the prospects for cultural diffusion with them? What about integration, or assimilation?

Since the arrival of the white man in the New World, a lot of water has flowed under the bridge—much of it polluted by social misunderstandings and ethnocentric bias. The ethics of feudalism had taken root in the whiteman's behaviour patterns; such ethos seemed to decree that might is right, and some colonizers spoke of a vague something they called "manifest destiny". It was assumed that the social patterns of Europe were basic to sensible human behaviour; therefore, all other social elements could, and should, be integrated and manipulated to that end. And they further believed that these ends could be accomplished by a type of thought control exercised throughout the administration of religious, business and educational institutions.

---

[1]Some conception of this time element can be gained, if we consider the physical adaptations alone. American Indians, for example, have markedly scooped-out, shovel-shaped incisor teeth as compared to the more rounded forms of white immigrants. In blood-group typing, the natives of South and Central America belong entirely to the "O" group. North of the Mexican border, 85—90 % are of this same blood group and the remainder are "A" group. None has "B" group, common to the rest of the world.

In academic circles, the theory was held (and widely propounded) that societies evolve from hunting, to pastoral stages, to agriculture; and from barbarism to some sort of glorious social state called "civilization". Western society, of course, securely ensconced at the top of the heap, could benefit from its position of cultural excellence. Recently, however, it has become apparent to many, that this type of nutritive pap may be wonderful food for the national ego, but it is also the verbal mash that feeds a monster called ethnocentric prejudice, or racism. After two hundred years of co-existence, many theorists are coming to see that forced integration does not work—that cultures can be overpowered and swallowed, but they do not necessarily digest.

Fortunately today, perspectives are widening. Social psychologists are beginning to examine and explain a natural process that takes place spontaneously, when peoples of any differing environmental background are thrown together.

The process of acculturation is simple, and it may be explained something like this: When two individuals or groups of individuals live together in close association for any length of time, they tend to develop traits of personality, behaviour, disposition and appearance that are common to all. This can be noted in simple family groups, in isolated rural communities, or even in city ghettos. What happens is that an internal cultural exchange takes place, a sort of social homogenization process that creates a new and more complex association. In other words, the flow of cultural contributions is a many-avenued thoroughfare.

The blinding prejudice of Western society toward Aboriginal cultures has often made racial empathy impossible. But, in spite of the barriers of snobbery, a great deal of acculturation has already taken place. Regardless of gratitude or ingratitude, our total society is the recipient of a great legacy from our brothers and sisters, the North American Native People. And, whether you know it or not, your lifestyle has been greatly influenced—and to your everlasting advantage—by input from the great Indian cultures of the past, to an extent that you will hardly credit.

When we say that acculturation is a many-avenued thoroughfare, some may ask, what have the *Indians* gained from this exchange? If it will help to understand the process, a few instances can be cited from the current scene.

We might note today, how the Indian people of this continent have become sufficiently conversant with the English language, that they are now able to use it as a common communications medium. Now, they are able to bridge the divisions caused through the multiplicity of their own languages and are thus able to organize themselves in Brotherhoods, Federations and Associations in order to further their own interests. Many Indians have mastered the technology of electronics to the point where they are able to operate radio programs, produce films, publish some first-rate Native newspapers and magazines, and communicate by satellite.

This represents one direction of cultural flow, and we hope that in the future, it will be possible for this flow to increase in avenues where it can be of mutual benefit. The purpose of this book however, is to focus upon the tremendous accultural benefits which have moved in the reverse direction. What advantages have accrued to Western society as a result of its contacts with the Native People of North America? Are we conscious and appreciative of these contributions? And if not, why not?

Industrial growth in the past half-century has been so rapid that some segments of society have become preoccupied with self-aggrandizement to the point that they have forgotten their own early beginnings. Then, too, the years of strife that accompanied the period of colonial incursion, have left unpalatable memories. Could it be that these factors tend to block out recognition of benefits gained by association with the original inhabitants?

But if there is any substance in these reasons, then the need for some reflection now becomes even more urgent if we are to understand our own identity. We may know who we were by reading history, but do we know who we have become? Tennyson, the British lyric poet, put these words in the mouth of the wandering Ulysses: "I am part of all that I have met."

Post script

When Columbus first met the inhabitants of the North American shores, he believed these people must have been made in the true image of God, *du corpus in deo*. Thus, *in deo* became *Indian*.

Ontario Indian (Vol. 5 No. 9) September 1982

1
CHAPTER

Name Calling Made Popular

As part of the landscape of southern Saskatchewan, there is a long valley which winds its way across the prairie to become part of the present Assiniboine River system. On the opposite side from B-Say-Tay point, there is a small town called Ketepwa. For centuries, the Plains-Cree had lived in this area, and because of the many echoes that would reverberate through the hills on a still prairie night, called their beloved valley *Ke-tep-wa*, "who calls?" French traders were so entranced by the name that they translated it into their own language and called it the Qu'Appelle Valley—also, "who calls?" in the French tongue.

Here, in our first paragraph, we have five place names that stem from Indian origins. We have also illustrated how a name can be juggled through a number of translations and still retain its original meaning.

Tribal names have always been both a source of interest and sometimes confusion to people who try to unravel them. But they are important because they are labels that symbolize identity. Place names, words used by the Native Peoples to identify themselves, and even the names they gave to inanimate objects, are also important to us now because many of them form a colorful part of everyday language.

Even the confusion is interesting, because this strange potpourri of identity labels makes an ideal place to launch our examination of human acculturation.

To get to the base of this confusion, and to clear the way for future discussion, it is necessary to understand some fundamentals. We must realize that the tribal societies of this continent were long in the making.

The native inhabitants were divided into a multiplicity of distinct societies that ran well over six hundred in number—about fifty tribes in Canada alone. These had developed from the basic language stocks[2] and constituted many related tongues and dialects. Then, each of these groups adopted a name by which they wished to identify themselves. To these we add the names that other tribes dubbed onto them (some complimentary, and some otherwise). And to complete the confusion, there were the names given to these tribes by newly arriving Europeans, themselves speaking a multiplicity of languages.

To illustrate the point, let us look at a few examples. One important group of Indians, speaking a common tongue, called themselves *Oceti Shakowin* "the seven council fires." A branch of this linguistic family called themselves, the Dakotas, meaning "the allies". But the French chose to bastardize an Algonkian term meaning "enemy serpent", and called them the Sioux.

Members of the Blackfoot Confederacy were given that name because their moccasins were dark in color, supposedly from running through burned grass after prairie fires. Another tribe from this group was called the Bloods by the English, though they still choose to refer to themselves as the *Kainai*.

One division of the Nadene family called themselves Dine, or simply "the People". But (and in spite of the fact that it was almost impossible for these people to pronounce a "V") the Spaniards called them the Navajos. And today, the northern contingents of this same Nadene linguistic family in the Arctic Regions of Canada (the Yellowknife, Dogrib, Kutchin, Beaver, Hare, Chipewyan and others) are still attempting to establish themselves as a self-governing entity in the name of the Dene Nation. These people have not forgotten who they are.

---

[2]Linguist, Edward Sapir, in 1929, was able to arrange them into six major groups. Clark Wissler in *Indians of the United States*, presents his entire discourse around these linguistic families, thus acquainting his readers with a clearer picture of who is who.

Another group, composed of five nations, speaking a kindred tongue and living in the Finger Lakes area of what is now New York State, called themselves the *Hotinonshonni* . But the French convinced the Algonkians that these were a hostile people, so should be known as the Iroquois, a word having reference to snakes. In an area bounded by Georgian Bay, some rivers called the Sturgeon, Severn, Nottawasaga and Lakes Bass and Couchiching, another member of this same Iroquoian family called themselves the *Wendots* and their homeland *Wendake* (wen-daw-kay), which meant, "a land surrounded by water." But the French called them Hurons from the French word, "hures" because of their hairstyle reminded them of the head of a wild boar. Not too charitable a name for an ally, but all part of the process.

In the same way, another group called themselves the *Lenni Lenape* or "the real people", but the English called them the Delaware. In the early times, the Cree referred to the people of the High Arctic as Eskimos, meaning "the eaters of raw fish". The Arctic people retaliated by calling the Cree *Itquilits*, meaning "the lousy ones". Today, in this era of ethnic sensitivity, both Cree and English have agreed to be more respectful and refer to these dwellers of the great white north by their self-chosen name, the Inuit.

But, regardless of all this confusion of cross-cultural name- calling, many of the original Indian designations have remained. Some tribal names such as: MISSOURI, MASSACHUSETTS, DAKOTA, ILLINOIS, KANSAS, UTAH, WYOMING, NEVADA and OHIO were appropriated to become the names of states. American cities too adopted the names of Indian tribes: MIAMI, MENOMINI, CHEYENNE, NATCHES, OSAGE and OMAHA for example. But the number of United States cities and towns of general Indian derivation would fill a volume and will not be attempted here; just a further smattering might include names like CHICAGO, MOBILE, MINNEAPOLIS, SEATTLE, KALAMAZOO, HACKENSACK, PONTIAC, TALLAHASSEE, OSHKOSH and many, many more.

If we were to take a map of North America today, it would be difficult to put down the point of a pencil without stirring up some hidden meaning enshrined there by Native imagery. To translate these names makes them come alive: ALABAMA, "the place where we rest" (Muskhogean); ACADIA, "the fertile land" (Micmac); ALASKA, "the peninsula part" (Aleut); MENOMINEE, "place of wild rice" (Ojibway); OKLAHOMA is a

Choctaw word for "red man", and UTAH is a name the Utes gave themselves. Most of these names have a message to convey and some of the results are humorous. If the meaning is complimentary, like TORONTO, which means, "gathering place", then the Chamber of Commerce is quick to herald the message. If, on the other hand, the name does not carry a suitable message, like CHICAGO (which, in the Miami tongue, means, "the place of skunks"), the derivation is conveniently lost in the mists of time. It should be pointed out in passing however, that the Miami tribe regarded the skunk as a gentle member of the animal kingdom, who demanded respect and was not to be easily pushed around.

A Sampling of Canadian Place Names

Because of limited space, it is not possible to make a thorough list of place names to include Mexico, Central America, the United States and Canada. Possibly, it would give some idea of the extent of this contribution if we made a very limited survey of the Canadian territory alone. Place names become a spiritual part of the toponomy of each country. The Indian names appear to carry a certain brooding mysticism.

The name, CANADA, itself is thought to be a version of the Iroquois word *ken-a-tah*, which referred to "a cluster of dwellings". To the Indians, it was possibly a word of trifling importance, but to the French, who were hearing it for the first time, it seemed eminently appropriate. Then, there are such names as: SASKATCHEWAN, MANITOBA, QUEBEC, ONTARIO and YUKON—all with a beautiful lilt that gives them a uniquely Canadian flavour. SASKATCHEWAN is taken from the Cree word, *kisiskatchewani* which means "swift flowing river"; MANITOBA could come from the Assiniboine dialect, *mini-tobow*, "lake on the prairie" or the Cree expression, *maniot-wapow*, referring to a strait watched over by the spirit of the Great Manitou; QUEBEC is from the Algonquian word, *kebec*, meaning "where the water narrows"; ONTARIO was named indirectly by the Hurons who referred to the lake as, *ouitario*, meaning "beautiful, sparkling water"; and YUKON is from the Athapascan word, *diuke-on*, for "clear water".

Then, there are names to indicate special religious significance. MANITOULIN ISLAND, for example, is the "home of" the Great Manitou or, putting it in the English vernacular, "God's Country". MANITOU BEACH, in Saskatchewan, praises the same divinity. MEDICINE HAT, in Alberta, is named after the *saamis* of the Blackfoot tribe, which is the headdress of the medicine man. SPIRIT RIVER is translated as the Cree word, *chip-si-pi*. The MISSINAUBI RIVER refers to reflections of pictographic messages from the rocky banks to the water below. And SQUAMISH, B.C., means, "mother of the winds". All of these meanings carry their own message of reverence.

So many of the names we have adopted for our lakes and rivers have a special quality that is hard to describe. They are musical, and they flow with such grace that they carry an enchantment, even though we may not be aware of their meaning. Let us pick a few and explain the hidden message: SKEENA (Salish) "out of the clouds"; SAGUENAY (Cree) "water that goes out"; MINNEDISA (Sioux) "swift water"; WINNIPEG (Cree) "muddy water"; WINNIPEGOSIS (Cree) "little muddy water"; PETIT-CODIAC (Micmac) "the river that bends round back"; PASSAMAQUODDY (Penobscot) "where the fish leap out of the water"; PETITSIKAPAU LAKE (Nascapi) "willow fringed"; UPSALQUITCH (Micmac) "whimpering as it goes along"; RESTIGOUCHE (Micmac) "good river"; ATTAWAPISKAT (Ojibway) "at the mouth"; NIAGARA (Huron) "thunder of waters". This small sampling of names, taken from the Canadian water systems, tells a brief but descriptive story, from "whimpering streams" to "thundering waters".

But Indian imagery related to water flow is not restricted to the names of rivers alone. The toponomy of Canadian towns and cities has been influenced by Indian names associated with water systems. If the readers would like to test their knowledge of Canadian geography, try this. From the information, first guess the province and, if you are really good, you may be able to name the water intimated. Try these names: KAMLOOPS (Salish) "a meeting of the waters"; PUGWASH (Micmac) "shallow water or shoal"; KAPUSKASING (Cree) "place where the river bends"; TIMAGAMI (Ojibway) "deep water"; MATTAWA (Algonquin) "confluence of rivers"; MATACHEWAN (Cree) "meeting of the currents"; CHICOUTIMI (Montagnais) "end of deep water"; CAUGHNAWAGA (Iroquoian) "rapids in the river"; COATICOOK (Abenaki) "river of pine land"; MAGOG (Abenaki) "expanse of water"; TEMISCAMING (Cree) "deep water"; WAKAW (Cree) "crooked lake"; TUCKET (Micmac) "great forked tidal river"; ABITIBI (Algonquin) "half-way water"; MISSISSAUGA (Mississauga) "river having several outlets"; OSHAWA (Seneca) "crossing of a stream"; PETAWAWA (Algonquin) "where one hears water far away".

Then, how about places that are named because of some particular feature of topography that ties it to a location? Lacking tourist maps and guide books, the original Canadians attached name tags highlighting certain physical features. Here is a representative list, some of which you will recognize. There is GRAND MANAN ISLAND, from the Malecite word, *Munanook*; SIOUX LOOKOUT, a high promontory where the Ojibway watched for the Sioux; ABEGWEIG PASSAGE, from the Micmac meaning, "lying parallel with the land", their name for what is now Prince Edward Island; UNGAVA, the Inuit word meaning, "far away"; WABANA, the Micmac name for Belle Isle; GASPE, the Micmac word for "end of the extremity"; and places like, MOOSE JAW, which has nothing to do with a moose's jaw whatsoever, but comes from the word, *moosgaw*, referring to the warm breezes created by the sheltering banks of a small prairie escarpment. Other names might include: CHILLIWACK, "going back up"; ESQUIMALT, "a place gradually shoaling" COUCHICHING, "a group of pine trees"; GANANOQUE, "rocks rising out of the water"; SHAWINIGAN FALLS, "portage on the crest"; or TADOUSSAC, meaning, "female breasts" and referring to well-rounded hills in the area.

Shall we proceed? There is IGLULIK, (Inuit) for "an abundance of igloos"; KEEWATIN (Cree) for "north wind"; WADENA (Ojibway) "a little round hill"; MANKOTA (Sioux), "deposits of earth pigment"; BATISCAN (Montagnais) "light mist"; THE PAS (Cree) "narrows between high banks" from the word *opaskweow*; NIPIGON (Ojibway) "continuous water"; MICHIPICOTEN (Algonquin) "place of bold promontories"; and POWASSAN (Ojibway) "big bend". Then, there is a long list of colorful Micmac names, a few of which are CHIGNECTO, "the great marsh country"; BUCTOUCHE, "big bay"; CHEBUCTO BAY, "a bay running far back"; ANTIGONISH, "where the branches are torn off"; MEMRAMCOOK RIVER, "all spotted stones"; BEDEQUE, "place on backward turn of river"; and ANNIEOPSQUATCH, "rocky mountains". Or, how about such names as, PENETANGUISHENE, meaning "a place of white falling sand"; AQUATHUNA COVE, the Beothuk word for "white rock or grindstone". But, possibly the distinctive name of all, and the least apt to be approved by any chamber of commerce is the name, POVUNGNITUK which, to the Inuit, means "place of bad smells".

The Native People of Canada were almost completely dependent upon a food supply found growing wild in nature. They were, therefore, intimately familiar with their hunting grounds, and named places where game and fruit could best be taken. We have appropriated many of these names. Consider these locations for the harvesting of fruit, for example: SASKATOON (Cree) "berries from a shadbush"; PEMBINA (Cree) "water berries"; MOOSOMIN (Cree) "high bush cranberries"; LILLOOET (wild onions); SHUBENACADIE (Micmac) "a place where ground nuts grow". Or these places to catch fish, COQUITLAM (Salish) "small red salmon", sockeye; GOGAMA "fish leap over surface of water"; JOGGINS (Micmac), "a place of fish weirs"; LAC MEGANTIC (Abenaki) "place of many fish"; or QUALICUM BEACH, "where you find dog salmon". Still, other places were known for game, places like MIMICO "place of wild pigeons"; SHIPPEGAN (Micmac), "a small passage ducks fly through"; AKPATOK (Inuit), "place of birds"; ANTICOSTI (Iroquoian) "hunting ground for bear"; CACOUNA (Cree) "home of porcupine"; and METANE (Micmac), "beaver pond"; AKLAVIK (Inuit), "where there are bears"; PANGNIRTUNG (Inuit), "place of the bull caribou". Or, there were places that singled out one animal as a symbol, places like PONOKA, which simply means, "elk" in Blackfoot; KELOWNA, meaning "grizzly bear"; WAWA, meaning "wild goose" in Ojibway; WABUSH, meanig "rabbit" and WAWANESA is Cree for "wild Goose".

But, aside from game, the Indian people were always in search of raw materials with which to fashion their tools and supplies. A limited list might include MANICOUAGAN (Cree), "where there is canoe bark"; MISSISQUOI (Abenaki), "place where flint is found"; LAC ETCHEMIN (Abenaki), "where there are hides to make snowshoes"; ATIKOKAN (Ojibway), "caribou bone"; RIMOUSKI (Micmac) "land of moose". Then to top it all off, there was the NASS RIVER area, which the Tlingits have called, "a food depot", and NEEPAWA, which translates as "the home of abundance or plenty."

From the foregoing, it is apparent that much of the toponomy has resulted through adaptations to Indian labeling initiative. It is, therefore, gratifying to note instances where the reverse has happened—where whitemen have enshrined the memory of Indian people and tribes in more recent designations. Consider place names like, DESERONTO, a great Mohawk Chief; MUSKOKA, a Huron dignitary; DONNACONA, the Huron Chief taken on a visit to France by Jaques Cartier; PIAPOT, a Cree Chief who defied intruders in Saskatchewan; SHANADITHIT BROOK in Newfoundland, named after the last living Beothuk; or, in lighter vein, a local Cree dwarf called, KAMSACK, which translates as "the big man".

Other references to people will include: ASSINIBOINE, Siouxan tribe noted as "stone boilers"; SHUSWAP LAKE, after a noted Salish tribe; OT-
TAWA, for an Algonquian tribe known as the Odawas; KOOTENAY, for the famous "water people"; KITLOPE LAKE, where the Kwakiutl people were known as, "the people of the mountain pass"; and OKANAGAN, where a Salish tribe could see "the top or head of a certain mountain".

Of recent years, the designations of large areas to wilderness and recreation has called for the naming of National and Provincial Parks. Here, too, Indian names have been appropriately selected; preserves like ALGON-QUIN PARK, named after a leading linquistic family; YOHO NATIONAL PARK, Cree for "how wonderful!". KEJIMKUJIK PARK, Micmac for "an attempt to escape"; NAHANNI PARK, named for Athapascan "people of the west"; MACTAQUAC PARK, where the Malecite people noted "the big branch"; ANYUITTUQ NATIONAL PARK in the Arctic Regions, which the Inuit appropriately call, "the land of the big ice"; KOUCHIBOUGUAC PARK, in New Brunswick where the Micmacs referred to "the long tidewater river"; WOOLASTOOK PARK, which was the Malecite name for St. John River; and even TRACADIE, Micmac for "camping ground", and MALAGASH - Micmac for "place of games". And this is only a scattered glimpse of Canadian geography.

The list seems to go on indefinitely and as it does, the search becomes more fascinating. As we become familiar with the names and their background meaning, we gain a new appreciation of the people and events that preceded us. We tend to learn history and geography simultaneously. The mixing of races and cultures is acculturation in action. Many names are direct translations, some are perceived meanings of an unfamiliar tongue, but still others illustrate what happens when amalgamations take place.

ECUM SECUM for example, is a corruption from Micmac that almost defies meaning; ALGOMA is a mixture of English and Ojibway compounded by the noted ethnologist, Henry Schoolcraft, combining "Al" from Algonquin with the Ojibway word, "goome" meaning lake; MUS-QUODOBOIT is an even more complicated amalgam of French, English and Micmac in a phonic goulash, which is said to mean, "rolling out in foam". Possibly the authors for the name FORT CHIMO, on the bottom end of Ungava Bay, had a better ear for audio frequency modulation when they mixed some Indian and Inuit sounds together to get a name meaning "good cheer".

Augmenting the English Vocabulary

Place names as we can now appreciate, tend to become anchored to specific areas as identity tags. But how about the larger field of language? What about multi-lingualism?

To the first European adventurers to settle in the Americas, Spanish, French and English were the principal languages. Some of the more scholarly newcomers were bilingual, the very clever might be conversant in three languages, but the majority were limited to the use of their mother tongue only. Thus, it came as some surprise to find many Indians conversant in several Native languages (of which there were eleven language stocks in Canada alone, plus dozens of dialect variations). As an added vehicle of communication, a thoroughly effective system of sign-language served as an umbrella device.

What is interesting here however, is the number of Indian words that have found their way into all three of the imported languages and found a permanent place in the European lexicon. For the purpose of the accounting, let us consider some of this transfusion to the English dictionary.

Visitors to a new land are primarily interested in the people they encounter, the clothes they wear, the tools and technology they have created. Thus we have such words as:

CANOE	(Carib:*canoa*) — a light boat to paddle
DORY	(Central America:*dori*) — a small dugout fishing boat
HAMMOCK	(Arowakan:*hamaca*) — a swinging bed
KAYAK	(Inuit) — closed-in canoe

PIROQUE	(Carib) — a boat made from a hollowed log
TOBOGGAN	(Abnaki:*udabagan)* — a long sled without runners
TOMAHAWK	(Algonquian) — a light axe
ULU	(Inuit) — a special shape of knife
UMIAK	(Inuit) — a large skin boat
PAPOOSE	(Algonquian) — baby
PEEWEE	(Massachusett) — very small
SQUAW	(Massachusett) — wife or woman
ANORAK	(Inuit) — warm jacket
MOCCASIN	(Narragansett:*moccussin)* — footwear
PONCHO	(Arouchan) — shoulder shawl

The houses and shelters these people occupied were known variously as HOGAN (Navaho); KIVA (Hopi); SHACK (Nahuatl); WIGWAM (Ojibway); and WICKIUP (Fox). TEOCALLI (Nahuatl) referring to the temple at the top of truncated pyramids, is still used in Mexico.

The landscape and even the weather have given us some new words for our vocabulary. Words likeBAYOU (Choctaw) a marshy inlet; CHINOOK a warm winter wind in the West. MUSKEG (Ojibway) a thick layer of decaying vegetation; HURRICANE (Arawakan) *hurakan* a violent windstorm.

Animals generally, were a source of interest to newly arriving Europeans, for there were many species here with which they were unfamiliar. Accordingly, they adopted the Indian names as part of their education. Here is a sample list:

CACOMISTLE	(Nahutl) — a slender, racoonlike animal
CARIBOU	(Algonquian:*kaleboo)* — North American reindeer
CAYUSE	— Oregonian name for a small pony
COUGAR	(Tupi) — means, "false deer" in reference to its colour.
COYOTE	(Nahuatl) — named after thorny bush called "coyotilla"
COYPU	(Araucan) — a water rodent called, "nutria" in U.S. and Canada
COATI	(Tupi) — a small member of raccoon family
JAGUAR	(Tupi) — a large member of the leopard family
KINKAJOU	(Tupi) — a jungle animal of raccoon family

MOOSE	(Massachusett:*moos*) — means "eats off"
MARGAY	(Tupi) — small type ocelot
MALAMUTE	— type of dog familiar in Arctic
MANATEE	(Carib) — an aquatic mammal from the tropics
MUSQUASH	(Abnaki) — sometimes called a muskrat
OPPOSUM	(Indian name origin in dispute)
PACA	(Tupi) — a tailless rodent of Central America
PECCARY	(Carib) — a tropical piglike animal
PEKAN	(Abnaki:*pecane*) — an animal of the weasel family
RACCOON	(Algonquian:*arakunem*) — appropriately means "the hand scratcher"
SKUNK	(Abnaki:*segoku*) — a musky-smelling, striped animal
TAMANDUA	(Tupi:*tapyra*) — a hoglike American mammal
TAPIR	(Tupi) — a small, tree-dwelling anteater
WAPITI	(Shawnee) — deer or pale-colored elk
WOODCHUCK	(Chippawa:*weotchek*) — sometimes called groundhog

And let us continue this list of zoological specimens by including birds, reptiles and fish:

CONDOR	(Quechua) — a large vulture
GUAN	(Carib) — a large bird of Central America
HOATZIN	(Nahuatl) — a tropical tree-climbing bird
JUBIRU	(Tupi) — a wood ibis found in tropics
JUCANA	(Tupi) — a water bird found in tropics
QUETZAL	(Nahuat) — a brilliantly coloured bird from Mexico
SORA	— a wading bird of the rail family
TANAGER	(Tupi:*tangara*) — a scarlet coloured bird, a summer visitor to Canada.
TINAMOU	(Carib) — a bird of the partridge family from Central America.
WHISKYJACK	(Cree) — etymologized from Weesaukejauk, a legendary prankster, also known as Canada Jay.
AXOLOTL	(Nahuatl) — a small type of edible salamander
IGUANA	(Arawakan) — a large tropical lizard
MENHADEN	(Narragansett) — a small fish used for oil and fertilizer

MUSKALL-UNGE	(Algonquian:*mas* *"great"* plus *kanonge*) — a large type pike
ONANANICHE	(Algonquian) — a type of salmon
SCUP	(Narragansett) — fish related to snappers
TERRAPIN	(Algonquian) — a diamond-backed turtle on the Atlantic Seaboard
TULLIBEE	(Cree) — a kind of whitefish found in the Great Lakes

Then, throughout the Americas there was a long list of trees and botanical species that were different and needed names. The Indians supplied them. For example:

CHICKLE	(Nahuatl:*chancli*) — tropical plant used for making chewing gum
CATALPA	(Creek:*katuhlpa*) — a variety of tree grown in southern U.S.
CEIBA	(Arawakan) — a tropical tree yeilding kapok
CHINQUAPIN	— a nut tree related to the chestnut
CHILI	— a pepper which grows red pods
COHUNE	— a feathery palm of Central America. Good for nuts, lumber and oil.
COCAO	(Nahuatl:*cocautl*) — name of tree which produces Cocoa seeds
COONTIE	(Seminole:*kunti*) — tropical plant with starchy roots
GRUGRU	(Carib) — name of tropical palm. Also, grugru worm.
GUAVA	(Arawakan) — fruit bearing tree of tropical America.
MANIOC	(Tupi) — also called cassava. Roots produce tapioca
MESQUIT	(Nahuatl:*mizquitl*) — spiny tree or shrub of Texas and Mexico
MAIZE	(Taino or Arawakan) — now known as corn
MANGROVE	(Taino) — tree which grows in swampy tropics
OCOTILLO	(Nahautl) — a desert plant
PAWPAW	(Carib) — produces papaya fruit
SEGO	(Shashonean) — a bulb plant found in southwest
PECAN	'(Algonquian) — tree producing olive-shaped nut
SAPADILLA	(Nahuatl:*tzapotl*) — an evergreen yielding sapota fruit

SASKATOON	(Cree:*misaskwatomin*) — berry-yielding tree sometimes called, shadbush
SASSAFRAS	(Indian and Spanish mix) — bark of roots used to make medicine
SQUASH	(Massachusett:*askoot-asquash*) — member of the gourd family
TULE	(Nahuatl) — a large bullrush
TOBACCO	(Carib:*tobako*) — a plant of the nightshade family
TOMATO	(Nahuatl):*tomatl* — yields red fruit with juicy pulp
TAMARACK	(Algonquian) — a feathery evergreen, abundant in Canada
TUPELLO	(Muskhogean) — a gum tree of southern U.S.
WICOPY	(Cree:*wikiyap*) — leatherwood or basswood tree
WAHOO	(Creek and Dakota) — a softwood good to make arrows

From these trees, shrubs and plants, of course, they prepared foods which the new arrivals found quite palatable. These are examples:

COCOA	(Nahuatl) — a chocolate drink made from cacao buds.
PEMMICAN	(Cree) — a food prepared from fruit, meat and suet.
PINOLE	(Nahuatl:*pinilli*) — flour made from corn and mesquit beans
PONE	(Algonquian) — bread, like in corn pone
TUCKAHOE	(Algonguian:*tuckawhoughe*) — truffle made from an underground fungus
TAMALE	(Nahuatl) — a meat, pepper and corn mixture that is a Mexican staple today
TAPIOCA	(Tupi) — made from casava or manioc roots

There were drugs and medicines to be made from the various plant species, so a partial list will suffice here. Also, let us include some materials used for utility purposes.

CURARE	(Tupi) — a drug extracted from the root of a tropical plant.

COHOSH	(Algonquian) — a group of herbs used in medicine
HOOCH	(Tlingit:*hoochinoo*) — slang word for homebrew
IPICAC	(Tupi:*ipekaaquene*) — roots of a plant used to stop diarrhea
MESCAL	(Nahuatl:*mexcelle*) — a liquor made from the fermented juice of agave
PEYOTE	(Nahuatl) means "caterpillar" — made from mescal cactus of Mexico
PIPISSEWA	(Cree:*pipisisikweu*) — plants used as diuretic and tonic
PULQUE	(Mexican Indian) — fermented juice of amerillis (agave)
QUININE	(Quechua) — anti-malaria drug extracted from cincona bark
TACAMAHAK	(Nahuatl:*tecomahea*) — a strong, smelly resin used in ointments.
COPAL	(Nahuatl:*copalli*) — a resin used in varnishes
HENEQUEN	(Arawakan) — a fiber plant used to make fertilizer
GUANA	(Quechua) — bird dung collected for fertilizer
SISAL	(Maya) — the fiber from agave in Yucatan. Used for making rope.

From the foregoing examples, it becomes apparent that Native Indian contributions to the English word-bank have been substantial and widespread. Identification labels have been adopted from the many northern tribes, but the reader will notice that many have been included from southern language groups as well. Nahuatl, which is the spoken language of the Aztecs, has been a big contributer to the Spanish that is spoken in Mexico, but it has augmented the English lexicon as well. Then we have several words from the Tupi language of the lower Amazon and Quechua which was dominant in the land of the Inca, just to add spice and to show how widespread this assimilation has been.

In addition each term is almost invariably related to the ecological scene. Indians lived as one with the forests, mountains, prairies and lakes, in an intimate relationship. They studied animals closely and knew their ways, respected the unseen powers of the wind and storms and were thankful for the stocks of food that were placed upon the earth for all to share. It was from these sources that Indians drew their picturesque phrases so liberally laced with metaphors, similes, mimicry and humour.

Even in the naming of their children, Indians showed this relationship with nature. Every baby had an identity and might be named a Spotted Fawn, a Babbling Brook, a Downy Feather or a Wounded Rabbit. And they grew up to be stalwart men, sachems, and mothers, such as Sacajawea, Big Bear, Crowfoot, Red Cloud, or Sitting Bull.

In this setting and with this background, it is difficult to understand why Hollywood, for the past half-century, has attempted to stereotype Indians as taciturn character-types who make such phonic utterances as, "HOW" and "UGH"—sounds seldom heard by real, live Indians anywhere. Possibly the ersatz film version is only a reflection of Hollywood's own rejection of *homo sapiens* as creatures of nature.

2

CHAPTER

The Gift of Survival

In this modern era of ideological politicking and sophisticated weaponry, people of the Western cultures tend to meet any outward visitations of their domain with a knee-jerk reaction of perceived danger. The first impulse seems to decree that newcomers be greeted with "a show of force". Thus, we muse about "a clash of the planets", "a war of the worlds", or "hostile visitors from outer space". No craft from Mars, or any other celestial body would be likely to land at LaGuardia or Toronto Island airport without causing great consternation and being met by an impressive array of military hardware. But it was not so with the Indian societies, and there is possibly no better example of this facet of human behaviour to illustrate the difference in social attitudes of the two cultures toward all living creatures.

When Columbus arrived in the islands of the Caribbean, with his sailing craft, metal guns and trained domesticated horses, we can be sure that it was no less of a visual shock to the Arawak Indians who were waiting on the shore; to them he could well have been from outer space. Yet this did not diminish the warmth of their welcome. The newcomers were an aggregation of bewildered souls who thought they had landed in India. But they were met by a group of singing, dancing people whom some imagined to be the fabled dryads mentioned by ancient poets. As Columbus wrote in his journals: "The people of this island, and all others I have found and seen, are artless and generous with what they have, to such a degree as no one would believe but he who has seen it."

With these thoughts in mind, can we speculate what the future might have been had Columbus and other adventurers been met with open hostility on all fronts? Possibly the process of acculturation might have been halted before it could get started, or terminated altogether.

However, it seemed to be the nature of the Indian personality to be curious, friendly and hospitable as a prime and basic response. So, in addition to the promise of an abundant food supply (which we will deal with in a later chapter), the newcomers were to receive the precious gift of survival.

*   *   *

When the Portuguese explorer Gaspar Corte-Real, landed on the shores of Labrador in 1501, he did not exactly endear himself to the band of Naskapi Indians who greeted him. Their hospitality and goodwill were rewarded by a sullen Latin shrug as a group of fifty-seven Natives were ushered aboard his ship to be sold as slaves in Europe. The Peninsula of Labrador, thus carries a name which, when translated loosely from the Portuguese language means, "a place to get cheap labour."

A few years later, when the more genteel Jacques Cartier entered the wider St. Lawrence estuary and dropped anchor in the Bay of Chaleur, he and his men were greeted by Indian woodsmen in a display of great jubilation. Canadian historian Thos. B. Costain, in his book *The White and the Gold*, recounts how Indians "brought cooked meats with them which they broke in small pieces on squares of wood; and then withdrew to see if their offering would be accepted." And further that they "dance exuberantly" and "uttered loud cries of astonishment and delight" at the texture and design of the visitor's costumes.

When English settlers arrived on the Atlantic seaboard, they were taught how to plant and cultivate corn and other crops. They were introduced to a new method of fertilizing the soil to stimulate growth. By planting the carcass of a dead fish in each hill, yields of this new field crop could be greatly increased. They were also shown some interesting methods of preparing food on the seashore; fresh clams could be baked by hot sand in quick order. The application of certain animal fats to the exposed skin could protect against cold, sun and insect bites. And this was only the beginning of a long list of folk remedies and medicines.

Whether or not these aids to a better lifestyle were appreciated by the Pilgrims is not the point at issue. They certainly elicited few rewards; indeed, on many occasions the aggressive attitudes later shown by the intruders often resulted in bloodshed. But almost without exception, the initial meeting of Indians with the emissaries of the Old World was cordial. And despite difficulties, the gifts of survival continued to flow.

White men often hold Indian societies up to scorn for not having developed the use of the wheel. But was the wheel the most functional technical device to use in the North America of those days? In the northern and eastern forested areas in particular, most transportation had to be pursued through dense wilderness with its tangle of windfalls and granite ridges. Navigation by water was obviously a more efficient method of travel.

What was needed was a craft that could withstand the punishment meted out by tumbling rapids and turbulent streams, but still light enough to make the necessary overland portages possible. This craft would have to be made from easily available materials, be shallow of draft, readily maneuverable, and curved at the bow and stern to minimize drag. The bark canoe was an admirable adaptation.

Canoes were evolved to meet specific needs and they varied in materials used (most tribes of the great Algonquian family who inhabited the Canadian Shield area used birchbark, while the Iroquoian people used elm bark). But they all followed a similar pattern of construction. Taking all of these requirements into consideration, Fraser Symington, in *The Canadian Indian*, describes the Indian Canoe as representing "a monumental feat in environmental technology". Modern "wild-river" sportsmen still hold it in reverence for wilderness travel and still use another Indian innovation, the "tumpline", a strap which fits across the forehead, to make the canoe manageable on the portage. In the terminology of contemporary environmentalists, the Indian canoe could be highly rated as "appropriate technology".

Without Indian guides, the early explorers would have encountered almost unsurmountable difficulties in penetrating the interior. Paramount among these was the matter of temporary shelter. Many Indian bands were nomadic in the sense that they followed the game and the natural fruit crops as a way of life. They had to be able to throw up quick shelters from the available materials. Hunting lodges might consist of twigs and branches thrown over a framework of poles. Wigwams were made from arched green boughs and sheets of bark to keep out rain and wind. Wood dwellers like the Micmacs, Ojibway, Cree and Naskapi were masters at constructing such shelters. In winter they often made them sufficiently warm by just adding rush mattings and animal hides.

In the Northern taiga (short tree) country Chipewyan, Cree, Kutchin, Naskapi and others used the skins of caribou. Further south in the great boreal forest, the Ojibway, Montagnais, Algonquians and Mistassini Cree found moose and bear more plentiful, while the Iroquois (less nomadic) built longhouses that sheltered several families and acted as storage for corn and other winter food supplies. By contrast, the Plains tribes such as Blackfoot, Assiniboine, Cheyenne and Crow, followed the buffalo herds and developed what might be described as the first "portable home" by throwing hides over a conical frame of saplings. These tipi dwellings could be folded up and moved on at an hour's notice. In each case we have described, the environment dictated the design and individual construction.

But when the white adventurers reached the Pacific seaboard, they were in for some further surprises. Coastal tribes such as the Haida, Nootka, Kwakiutl, Tlinkit and others lived among the tall, straight-grained cedars and found methods to split these great trees lengthwise using axes made of basalt and jade rock. Huge plank dwellings graced many a cove in the land of the Haidas and their hand-carved totem poles erected in front, proudly declared the ancestral lineage of its occupants. The Interior Salish, on the other hand, lived in more mountainous regions, where they had to adapt to more rigorous winter conditions. Their houses were built over pits sunk about three feet into the earth and preferably on a hillside. The earth excavated from the ground was later thrown over a framework of poles covered with matting which constituted the roof.

In southern climates, of course, winter cold was not something to fear, so housing took other forms. The hogans of the Navajo people for example, were structures made of poles and chinked with mud. But other structures ranged from the simple adobe huts of the many desert tribes to the huge community complexes of stone and mud built into cliff sides by village dwellers in Pueblo country. The variations ran from this early version of high-rise living to the more down-to-earth bear grass wickiup of the Apaches.

When the white man ventured into the New World, he did not carry a credit card nor a letter of introduction to the nearest hotel in order to assure proper accommodation. No, he had a choice of building his own shelter or adapting the tried and tested methods of North America's indigenous peoples. No matter which choice he made, the Native model was there as a prototype. Whatever shelter he chose, he must have found the samples useful for he has gone so far as to enshrine such names as tipi, wigwam, kiva, hogan and wickiup in the English dictionary as part of his vocabulary. If the Indian bark canoe in the east was appropriate technology, so too, were the magnificent whaling boats carved out of tree trunks by Nootka and Haida fishermen of the Pacific Coast. The white man however, did not adopt these ocean-going craft because he had sailing vessels that he considered safer for longer voyages. This was not the case with the canoe. On the great St. Lawrence waterway the coureurs de bois and voyageurs expanded the smaller design into those huge freighter canoes, some carrying a load of five tons and manned by a dozen or so paddles. In these and other ways, as these European adventurers moved inland, they needed all of the innovative technology possible—and they found it among the Inuit and the Indians.

In the northern forest where the snow is deep, the white men saw their first snowshoes and toboggans.[3] The former were made from strips of wood, looped in different shapes and strung tight by lengths of animal gut or rawhide strips called *babiche*. These shapes vary from the wide-oval, bear-paw design of the Montagnais to the slim-oval, more pointed frame of the Swampy Cree. Each travelled a different terrain and each needed a suitable design. The toboggans were usually drawn by heavy draft dogs, a more rugged member of the species than those used to pull travois burdens across the prairie grasslands. The white man took to the new technology and has not diminished his interest to this day.

Both explorers and the settlers who followed were in constant need of appropriate clothing for rugged outdoor use. It did not take long to recognize the superior wearing qualities of buckskin jackets, fur-lined garments and moosehide moccasins. But in order to make these items, they first had to buy them or learn how to trap the fur bearers and to tan hides the Indian way; and they had to learn how to cut and sew these hides according to Indian patterns that had proven functional merit. The moccasin-toe design for footwear is still immensely popular and is worn today throughout the world. It is also recognized that a parka with wolverine fur trim around the

[3]Some specimens can be seen in the Ski Museum at Oslo, Norway.

face of the hood will not frost up like other furs. It must be remembered that first, all these furs had to be trapped and tanned, and that the Indians had a few unique trapping and tanning methods up their parka sleeves as well.

In the matter of providing clothing, there was much to learn about weaving throughout the continent. The Tlinkit and Tsimshian tribes on the Pacific Coast made blankets from the wool of mountain goats. The Salish weavers included dog hair, feathers and sometimes cedar bark. The Nez Perce or Shahaptin tribes and the Interior Salish extended the art further by weaving in strips of rabbit skin for added warmth. The Cordilleran Indians cut strips of muskrat, badger and beaver furs, then wove and laced them together to make capes that covered the entire upper body. It did not take the wandering adventurers too long to find the comfort in all of these creations. Indeed, the sportsman of today will still go out of his way to look through the markets of Vancouver and other coastal cities in search of those rugged, warm, jumbo-knit Cowichan sweaters still made by Native hands.

Making of clothing is an art in itself, but what about the instruments of the craft? Needles had to be made from bones, thread from roots and sinews, buttons from stones and other hard objects and straps cut from rawhide. Ingenuity was the watchword. Fraser Symington, in his book, *The Canadian Indian*, tells how the Cree and Saulteaux tribes used the penis bone of the marten for a needle, when they discovered that it had a natural eye through which to insert the thread. Knives and scrapers had to be devised from shale rock and obsidian outcroppings as there were no scissors. Combs were made from fish bones and teasel cones so that wool could be carded. Snow, cold, rain and calm—the indigenous people had to find methods to cope with the elements, and they were willing to share these with the newcomers.

When it came to facing bright, blinding snow, Native travellers devised goggles from flat pieces of wood, featuring a narrow slit for vision and blackened with charcoal to absorb the sun's rays.

Inter-tribal trade, to be sure, helped in making utility items more available. The distribution of flint is a case in point. From one source in the land of the Neutrals (now Southern Ontario) supplies are known to have been distributed as far west as the Rocky Mountains and north into the land of the Cree.

Food, shelter and clothing were the three essentials for these early white arrivals, but they would have been still in grave danger had they not received the willing assistance of competent Indian guides. Anyone living in the present era, who has had the experience of flying over the maze of lakes and rivers in the Lake-of-the-Woods district, west from Lake Superior, will wonder how anyone without maps or navigational instruments could have possibly found his way anywhere. Yet, such explorers as Brule and LaVerendrye penetrated these areas and continued so far west that they themselves did not know where they had been. These successes can be attributed only to the know-how of their many Indian advisors. The Lewis and Clark expedition, which made its way through the middle west into the Rocky Mountains and to the mouth of the Columbia River, is still the subject for volumes of historical adventure stories. The leaders of the expedition openly give credit in their journals to a Shoshoni woman named Sacajawea who acted as a guide and simultaneously nursed a two-month old baby.

Early visitors to the prairie country soon became aware of the fact that some food supplies must be stock-piled for days when hunting was poor, and that these supplies had to be portable and resistant to spoilage. Native people showed them how to make *pemmican*. Strips of lean buffalo meat were first hung over racks to dry in the air. Later, after pounding it to shreds, portions of melted fat were added, together with mashed saskatoon berries or similar tasty treats. The entire concoction was then worked into a homogenous mass and packed into conveniently sized bags made from green buffalo skin, lashed at the sides with rawhide lacing.

The nutritional value of this power-pack was high (one to two pounds per day was adequate to sustain an active woodsman on the move) and spoilage was minimal over extended periods of time. For all these obvious reasons then, pemmican became a staple. The Metis womenfolk became experts at preparing it in cakes and it came to be known as the "fuel of the fur trade."

For one race of people to be so generous with their worldly secrets was, in those days of European feudalism, a social phenomenon. But most important of all, a spirit of helpfulness attended these services. It is a factor which speaks highly for inherent Indian humanitarianism, even though it was not always graciously accepted. When the Spanish explorers, for example, decided to move up the west coast to California in 1602, the Carmelite friars who chronicled the expedition, spoke of "affable, generous Indians, friendly to the point of giving away whatever they had." Evidently, it was generosity of a new dimension—a few steps beyond Christian charity?

Further testimony to this inherent desire for mutual goodwill was the use of the *calumet* or "pipe of peace" throughout the Central Woodlands and prairie grasslands. Used extensively by such tribes as the Pawnee, Blackfoot and Sioux, these ornate pipes, decorated with feathers, sacred bones and tufts of hair, forestalled and eliminated many an act of violence. When the French entered the Mississippi country for example, they were received with the "dance of the calumet" ceremony which offered a degree of friendship beyond prudence. Although there may have been an aura of magic attached to the ceremony, there is no gainsaying the fact that good intentions were primarily indicated, fears of approaching strangers were put at ease and the stage was set for peaceful relations. The onus for civilized behaviour was on the visitors and too often they failed to recognize it.

The Urge To "Go Native"

To white pioneer stock (including women) living so close to nature was a temptation. Why not go all the way—join Native people and follow their lifestyle? Indeed, early colonial literature tells us of many who did succumb to the opportunity to literally "go native."

In the context of today's living, it is difficult for us to realize that life in the Indian encampments in those first days of Caucasian arrival was more sociable, more exciting and more soul-satisfying for the in-comer than the grim life on the frontier. Some sparsely settled white colonies tended to provide nothing but work for the men, lonely seclusion for women and in many cases, puritanical discipline for everybody. It is not surprising then, that many chose the more active centres of human association and refused chances to return to their own people after considerable pleading.

Of course, those who deserted the "civilized" state of enlightenment were looked on with scorn by their peers, and to return after a stay with the Native tribes was considered a laudable mark of triumphant good sense. Religious bias and the supercilious notion of racial purity, of course, were at the root of this kind of reasoning. Yet, despite the obvious ethnocentrism, many whites did make a lifetime career of going native! Some women who came into historic notice include personages such as Mary Jamieson, Mary Rowlandson and Frances Slocum, all of whom had the opportunity to be "liberated" but chose to remain as Indians.

Some sources point to the case of Cynthia Ann Parker who, in 1850, at the age of 13, was captured by the Comanches. When Cynthia grew older she became the wife of a chief and bore him children. Her brother discovered where she was living and undertook a "rescue" mission, but was surprised that she did not want to go. Accordingly she was kidnapped, but was so unhappy in her new captivity that she pined away and died. Then, there was the case of Mary Harris, who was taken captive at the age of ten. At the age of fifty, and happily married, she is reported to have said that she "wondered how the white men can be so wicked as I have seen them in these woods?"[4]

John Turner was a white man who could completely immerse himself in the Indian way of life and forget his Caucasian origins. We might also consider the life of John Logan, a man who is said to have been of full French blood. Captured as a boy, he was brought up as the son of a Mingo (Iroquoian) Chief and later became leader of the people who adopted him. In his adult life he lived and thought as an Indian and although forced into conflict with the whites, conducted himself with such dignity and integrity that Thomas Jefferson paid respect to his record; his oratory had been compared to the compositions of Cicero and Demosthenes. What is worth noting is that he could only have learned this art from his captors. Then, even in this twentieth century, we can point to a Canadian personality, Grey Owl, who was born in England but lived in Canada as Indian. Grey Owl so identified with the Native rhythms and harmonies that he was writing on the subject of ecology long before the meaning of the word was generally understood.

These, of course, are all cases where individuals have made their way into and been absorbed by Indian culture and societies. There are also examples from early times where mutual acculturation has taken place. Contact of the Quakers with the Cherokee Nation, for example, were perceived to be

[4]Christopher Gist's Journals

of mutual benefit to all concerned and cultural reciprocity was rapid. Thus, whereas De Soto had marched through the Cherokee territory at an early period and left little to remember but grief, the Quakers accepting the gifts of survival, gave benefits in return. According to Carl Wissler *(Indians of the United States)* census figures in 1825 recorded that there were 13,563 inhabitants in the Eastern enclave of the Cherokee Nation alone and of these 147 white men and 73 white women had settled down with Cherokee mates. Together, they built houses, established farm operations and planted forage crops for livestock. The social climate within the group was so conducive to creativity that unique cultural achievements appeared. A Native scholar by the name of Sequoia created an alphabet which made it possible to write the Cherokee language in phonetic symbols and within a short few years, the entire tribe was effectively literate.

When gold was discovered in the State of Georgia about 1828, everything changed for the Cherokees. Indian baiter Andrew Jackson, long known as a "borderer" (frontier smasher) now became U.S. President and set in motion the legal wheels of deception that saw the Cherokee Nation uprooted, and its tattered remnants marched to "Indian Territory" in Oklahoma—a dark chapter in the history of American democratic pluralism. In a modern context, twentieth century Canadians might consider the urgent concern for survival expressed by the Dene Nation in the Arctic regions since oil has been discovered in the Beaufort Sea.

*　　　　　*　　　　　*

For the past half-century, the progeny of immigrants to North America have lived a charmed life. We have lived off the bounty of the land and many have come to the conclusion that we no longer need the gifts of survival. We think that our own techniques are better. When the Machine Age arrived at our portals, perpetual prosperity was thought to be a foregone conclusion. In recent years however, all has not been sun and roses. The white man's economic institutions have been beset with problems of adjustment; the convulsive interruptions of recession, depression, deflation and inflation of the money supply have been punctuated by scares of pollution, war, crisis and nuclear destruction.

After World War II, the intellectual backwash of the cities began to congregate in "bohemian" communities in search of a new lifestyle. Many within this dissident set began to question the merits of the rush and turmoil existence as compared to Native Indian societies, who could not perceive that they were in any race with time. Some elements of the "counter culture", which arose after the early stages of this wave of revolt, felt an affinity for the unstructured lifestyle they thought existed among Native people. Now that modern technology has largely removed the burden of toil from the backs of the multitude they reasoned, there appears to be developing a general opportunity to escape to the more serene ways of life closer to nature. Some white people today, are beginning to wonder if they have somehow forgotten how to live. But, it is possible the gifts of survival have not all been given yet.

3

CHAPTER

Influences on the Sporting Tradition

"Hockey Night in Canada" has not always been a Saturday night fixture, nor did the players always wear such sophisticated paraphernalia as plastic helmets, shoulder pads and shin guards. These are some of the more recent refinements of the game. But what of the early origins?

Sports historians are hard pressed to find antecendents to many of the games we play today. Skirmishes we call "shinney" were played in many parts of the world and have had a strong influence on games that encourage team strategy, such as soccer and football. However, there are some cases where similarity of method and rule make the identification of origin more specific.

For example when George Becket, a white frontiersman, was roaming the prairie territory of the Blackfoot tribe in 1745, he reported seeing teams of young Indians playing a game which required a field about one hundred yards in length, featured a four-foot goal at each end, manned by ten to fifty players on each side, employed curved sticks made from wild red cherry wood and manipulated a "puck" made from hair-stuffed leather. Fan enthusiasm was not inflamed by dithyrambic sports announcers screaming "He shoots! He scores!", but the game does sound suspiciously like an early version of the game we call hockey.

Then there was a similar game played by the Teton-Sioux. They used sticks, a hard surfaced ball, and sometimes played on ice using two sharp pieces of buffalo shoulder-blade lashed to flat pieces of birchwood and securely fastened to the feet. This, too, gives every indication of being a forerunner to hockey.

John C. Ewart, eminent ethnologist, describes a ball game in which "as many as three hundred young men, divided into teams, chase a ball between goals set a quarter of a mile or so apart on a prairie or frozen river or lake. Hands could not touch the ball—a rough knot of wood, a rag filled buckskin bag, a hide-covered sphere. Like hockey players, they slammed the ball, and sometimes each other, with curved sticks."

Meanwhile, on the Atlantic seaboard, Micmac sportsmen were playing a game on the Dartmouth Lakes that afforded good recreation for dreary winter days. British soldiers from the garrison at Halifax were attracted to these events, and suggested that the game be livened up by putting it on metal skates which had been brought from Europe. According to Thomas H. Raddall, in *Halifax—Warden of the North*, the idea of pursuing the game on skates followed when troops were reposted to different places along the St. Lawrence waterway. A rousing game is reported to have taken place in 1855 at Kingston. In the meantime, the Indians at Dartmouth continued to oblige by supplying such tournaments with the proper sticks.

Long before this, during the French colonial administration centred at Montreal and Quebec, settlers noticed the Algonquian tribes playing another game using webbed sticks and featuring as many as 75 to 200 players at one time. The peculiar shape of these sticks reminded the settlers of a bishop's crosier, so the French called the game "lacrosse". However, this was not necessarily the place of origin for lacrosse. The Sioux played a version of the same game in the Central Plains many years previous. As a matter of record the Choctaw, a thousand or more miles further south, played a game using two smaller sized sticks with cradled ends. This leads many historians to believe that the game originally was played with a rubber ball and came from the sub-tropics. If this is the case, it only goes to show that history sometimes plays strange tricks. In Quebec, the "ball" that was used was usually made of compacted deer hair held together by thin strips of rawhide because rubber was not easily available. Because the northern tribes used the single "bishop's staff" with such vigor and enthusiasm, the game of lacrosse was selected as Canada's national sport at the time of Confederation. Some fans still think it should have been hockey.

Another case of where the "ball" won out over the "puck" was the early adoption of the game of volleyball. Cree athletes included both sexes as participants in this game which was played in open spaces anywhere. Two teams congregated in an area facing one another, boosted a fairly large ball into the air and engaged in a great display of dexterity, attempting to keep the ball from touching the ground within each team's designated territory. Is this the game that is played today in many gymnasiums and on strips of beach throughout the country in summer? You decide.

Northern tribes manufactured their own sports equipment and made their own local adjustments and rules. But influences and inspirations often have a way of filtering through from some fountain-head extraneous to the scene of action under study. In this case, it was the semi-tropical jungles of Central America.

In times, now ancient, the Olmecs lived in the Coatzacoalcos Valley of what is now Mexico. By the time of contact, they had developed corn as a field crop, domesticated many other wild plants, gathered chickle to make chewing gum and had coagulated the sap of certain trees by adding acids to make what we call rubber. The Olmecs and many of their neighbour nations were bouncing balls around long before the "Christian era". Hollow, bouncing balls were in general use throughout Mesoamerica long before Columbus was born. It is this ball in its many variations that made such an impact upon sporting events.

Aztec and Mayan athletes played out their sports spectaculars on great ball fields featuring a huge stone wall fitted with a fixed stone ring at its upper edge. The hard, rubber ball must pass through this hole for a score to be registered, and we can be sure that the bounce of the rubber was an important factor in making the game interesting. Today, some of our best and fastest games such as tennis, basketball and squash have been made better through the use of hollow rubber balls, and the game of golf relies on the hard, elastic core for distance and drive.

To Indian people, athletic prowess was always something to cultivate, and a source of pride. There were however, hundreds of games of a different nature; games just for the sheer enjoyment of play. The Lewis and Clark expedition of 1804 recorded in its chronicles some passages in reference to such pastimes. One paragraph states that: "They were seen to be playing a game with a strange wedge-shaped piece of wood, which was spun with string." In 1741, Manuel Quimper, a Spanish adventurer, had reported the same device in use. What they were describing was the spinning top, which gained great popularity among settlers and their children in years to come. Then there were rings-and-pins, bows-and-arrows, even dice. The game of hand was a favourite guessing game, while the spear-and-ring game was a favourite from Oregon country to the land of the Mandans. In the land of the Iroquois, a favourite winter sport was called snowsnake. A long trough was constructed along a course packed with snow, and contestants would line up at the starting post from which they would hurl a seven-foot stick. Distances of one-quarter mile and more were not unusual. It is interesting to note that this game is still an annual feature at the Six Nations Reserve near Brantford, Ontario.

These and other games, it would seem, were played for the sheer pleasure of the challenge. Thomas Morton, who lived with tribes along the Atlantic seaboard in the 1620's, described festivals where "they exercise themselves in gaminge, and playing at juglinge trickes, and all manner of Revelles, which they are delighted in, that it is admirable to behould what pastime they use, of several kinds, every one striving to surpasse the other, after this manner they spend their time...."

The archaic phraseology may be quaint to read now, but it reveals something about that pleasure facet of Indian sportsmanship. In a subtle way it explains something that other European immigrants marvelled at. Not only was the white man learning about new rules and equipment for the "gaminge" and "Revelles" as Morton called them, but the very spirit of the sport itself was worth noting and emulating.

There may be some scepticism on this point, on the part of North American citizens who have come to take everything for granted. So, let us whet our memories and consider European practices and attitudes in pre-Columbian days, or even pre-Frontenac times. What were they doing in England for sports entertainment? What was the main source of athletic enjoyment in Spain, or France, or Central Europe generally?

It would be wrong to suggest that there were none, for the gaming instincts of Europe were as active as elsewhere, but they were different. Some Europeans could read and write their various languages; great numbers could do simple arithmetic problems, so "parlor" games like checkers, cards, charades and chess provided plenty of mental stimulus. In the field of physical dexterity, however, their preference seemed to go to pastimes that were just a step away from the battlefield: sports requiring skills with weapons, such as fencing, javelin throwing and archery. By far the greatest interest in sports was focused on man's mastery over animals. Some students in the field of societal behaviour are beginning to ask if this is not a Biblical legacy of the Judeo-Christian ethic, which is set forth in the Book of Genesis in such words as: "Man was to have dominion over the fish of the sea and over the birds of the air and over everything that moves upon the earth." This could be interpreted as a license to dominate all "sub-species" as fair game.

There were spectator sports where animals were pitted against animals: fights promoted between savage dogs, or vicious encounters between specially bred fighting cocks, badger baiting and other similar practices. Some exhibitions featured man against beast, like fox hunts, where the quarry was pursued by a howling pack of hounds and a cavalcade of well-groomed horses directed by riders who were suitably attired both mentally and physically; or bull-fights, staged with all the pageantry and symbolism that could be mustered; or in extreme cases, humans of dissimilar ethnic stock (such as Beothuks of Newfoundland) were hunted for bounty. In many instances, public floggings, the burning of witches and public executions, although intended to convey lessons in social justice, took on the air of high entertainment for Europeans.

Remnants of these sporting spectaculars remain today in Western society, although they are losing favour with large segments of the public. Dog fights and cock fights have been promoted in North America in recent years in spite of legal blockages passed to stamp out such barbaric practices. Racoon baiting is still promoted as a "sporting" fixture in some American states and promoters have attempted to introduce it in Ontario. Bullfighting survives as a national "sports attraction" in Spain, Portugal and throughout the Latin parts of North and South America. Public executions, flogging and prisoner stonings are still practiced according to Islamic law in Saudi Arabia and other Muslim nations. The old concepts do not die easily.

It is not within the scope of our discussion here to explain why these attitudes persist in the Old World. What is important to this discourse is to point out that it would be virtually impossible for them to exist on a wide scale among Indian societies. Possibly the closest they came to this kind of behaviour was among certain societies of Mesoamerica (notably the Aztecs and Mayans) where human beings were sacrificed, not as punishment, but as a sacramental offering to the gods. The point of emphasis is that, deep within the psyche of most aboriginal tribes there has always been a world view which nurtured a respect for all living things, both plant and animal. The Christian psychology teaches that only man has a soul—the Indian holds that man, animal and plant possess life and that life *is* soul. They killed animals for food and clothing only. Students of Indian ethos and folkways agree that life was taken from the animal world almost apologetically, thanks for the sustenance was given to the Great Mystery or to the Spirit of the animal, and promises made that nothing would be wasted and the bones treated with respect. There was certainly no concept of "sport" involved.

So here we see a great divergence of attitudes—a difference that can be well illustrated when we consider what happens in the bushlands of the United States and Canada every fall with the opening of what has come to be known as "the hunting season".

At a time when the foliage has fallen from the trees, and natural cover is minimal, legions of urban-dwelling Nimrods enter the forests equipped with high-powered firearms, lures and other expensive paraphernalia and, in the spirit of high adventure, proceed to release their aggressive hostilities upon the wild creatures of forest and stream. Hunting lodges are well provisioned with processed foods, the atmosphere is festive and the male ego is fed with tall tales of imaginary triumphs highly laced with alcoholic stimulant. The trophy value of a stuffed head or a pair of antlers often outweighs the value of the meat. This "sport" is glamorized by a number of slick magazines and trade journals who are finding commercial outlets for bushwear and hunting gear. The various governmental agencies, who have the tourist trade in mind and licenses to sell, regard the scheduled slaughter in terms of a revenue industry.

It is true that some Indians today, because of economic circumstances, find themselves drawn into this seasonal hunting ritual as packers and guides, but in most cases their hearts are not in it. The conflict of cultural viewpoints puts the Indian in a position where he dares not be too vocal on such subjects, but occasionally someone will speak out loud and clear. Max Gros-Louis, co-author of *First Among the Hurons*, and himself a Grand Chief, is one of these. He refers to the days when he worked as a guide to surveyors and hunters in the Quebec woods in order to make a living and to improve his knowledge of the English language. He speaks of their utter naivety in the bush and of his difficulty sometimes, "to reply politely to those murderers who kill our game without eating it."

But whether the Indian hunter today is acting as a guide or hunting for food for his family, he is still in a bind. On the one hand, he is dependent upon the wildlife of the wilderness places for sustenance and he has been guaranteed hunting and fishing rights as recompense for surrender of other freedoms signed away in formal treaties. Yet he finds it most difficult to exercise these rights because of the hunting laws enacted by a dominant overseer. The fact of the matter is that the total population of immigrants to North America has grown enormously during the past three or four decades and many of these newcomers and their offspring want to hunt and fish, urged on by business interests who view hunting as an industry. The Native citizen, whose population figure is also expanding, finds his hunting territory infringed, his rights ignored and his needs misunderstood.

In this predicament, the Indian must sometimes fish beyond what is declared as "quota" or take game when a government agency has declared a "closed season". Local confrontations have taken place on issues ranging from fishing with the wrong kind of nets to harvesting frogs. And it is at these intervals, that the Indian brings down the condemnation of the white-faced lobby and even the criticism of some non-hunting conservationists (who have themselves been feeding well on pork and beef).

Some will conclude the Native People have forgotten their traditional concern for conservation. Acculturation works both ways! Others will point to the slaughter of buffalo in other times as an indication that this much-lauded "unity with nature" trait has been highly overrated. So, where lies the truth?

It is a fact, that before the arrival of horses and white men on this Continent, Plains Indians drove small groups of buffalo over cliffs and sometimes slaughtered more than they could eat. But, from the estimated four million buffalo roaming the grasslands in those days, the loss was insignificant. After the arrival of the horse, and a "scorched earth" military tactic of the invading whites however, this majestic species was brought to the edge of extinction by the year 1880.[5]

Much has been written on this subject, but simple arithmetic would exhonerate any serious complicity on the part of the Indians who, in the entire buffalo range, numbered less than 55,000 families. Since that era, Western society has added to its record by bringing so many species to the edge of oblivion, that today there is a rising concern in the Arctic for such animals

[5]See *the Canadian Indian* by: Fraser Symington - Chapter 18 - "The Big Buffalo Kill"

as the whale, walrus and Polar bear, to say nothing of the destruction of fish through the careless emission of industrial wastes into the water systems almost everywhere. Since the food supply of the general public has now come into question, many are starting to sit up and take notice.

The evidence appears to indicate that some changes have occurred in the white man's attitudes—and some have not. It becomes evident that, after four hundred years of contact with the Native People of North America, the spontaneous acculturation that has taken place has in some ways altered and mellowed many Old World concepts. The spirit of team-play has been heightened; the joy of outdoor living has become more real; the pleasures of lake and river swimming continues to be enjoyed; the whole concept that adults as well as children should play for fun and recreation, is growing into a generally accepted ethos which can be traced to the influence of America's First Citizens. The Indian Hall of Fame collects it celebrities from many tribes and many centuries. Some of the more recent additions might include such well known names as Tom Longboat, Jim Thorpe, Joseph Keeper Sr., George Armstrong, the Bentley Brothers, the Firth Sisters and many others. The sporting tradition is strong and is reflected in the names that many teams have adopted in order to bask in the prestige associated with such names, i.e. the Mohawks, the Detroit Redwings, the Edmonton Eskimos, and so on.

The white man has sampled some of the sporting traditions of the Indian societies and he likes them. Why then, does he not become magnanimous and accept the whole cloth?

Fun and recreation can be partners. The health-giving aspects are self-evident. Only in one field does it appear that the Indian concept has been resolutely overlooked. The white man remains adamant in his impression that the animal kingdom can be used as a pawn to satisfy certain primitive cravings for self grandiosity. When will he be able to decide which is fun and which is food—and differentiate? That can only come with a growing respect for the environment and for the life itself with which he must co-exist.

4

CHAPTER

The Gift of Better Health

In 1535, when the adventurous Jacques Cartier decided to spend his first winter in the Canadian woodlands, his concern about wilderness survival dwelt more on building palisades than on the more subtle imperative of proper nutrition. So when the winter cold arrived, and the snow drifted down, billowing into towering drifts, the small party of marooned foreigners began to realize that their greatest enemy was not lurking in the underbrush outside, but was attacking from within. Men contracted scurvy and twenty-five had died before Cartier decided to seek out some Indian help. Cartier reported that two women showed the visitors how to make a drink by boiling the bark and needles of a tree , and how this brew had sufficient vitamin content to restore the remaining crew to health. From that moment on, the gift of Indian medicine and health-knowledge would contribute toward a healthier Canada, and that contribution would extend to humanity at large.

Just how extensive this contribution has been is seldom appreciated but an honest recounting constitutes a story which is just short of incredible.

The typical tribesman of yesterday as we picture him in our minds, presents an imposing physique. He was erect, spare, athletic and lightly clothed. This is a true image. He walked quietly in the forest, stood proud among all men and was a statuesque figure on horseback. Today his imitators can be seen in the millions, wearing looser and more comfortable clothes, frolicking in the sun and naming their ball teams in subconscious admiration of the Indian tradition. In the intervening years, the white man has learned how to endure long journeys afoot; how to keep his body clean; how to use hundreds of indigenous plants to formulate creams and medicines, and a hundred and one ways to fend off disease, treat sunburn and protect the body from everything from chilblain to snakebite.

Personal Hygiene and the 'Sin' Syndrome

In the matter of personal hygiene, many present-day members of the social scene, who tend to entertain a degree of snobbery, will look at the record in disbelief. Now firmly in the grip of the commercials, warning of the shame of body odor, real estate under the fingernails, ring-around-the-collar, and hair on the legs, there is a tendency to stereotype Indians as being slovenly and dirty. In the modern setting, many whites fail to consider the squalid living conditions Indians are now forced to endure, and in the historic sense, they failed to distinguish between dirt and the smell of burning wood. So for the sake of clarity, let us look at the record. Possibly the right shoe sometimes finds itself on the left foot.

Whether or not the white man is prepared to admit self-delusion, his own written words tend to point in this direction. Records show that European arrivals in Indian territory were quite a smelly lot—and moreover, their kinfolk back in the homeland in those days were no better. We have only to read the descriptions of Anatole France and Charles Dickens to know that cleanliness was not one of their better virtues. We can read passages where the social elite found it necessary to drench their bodies with lotions and sweet-smelling waters in order to stifle body odors. The lower class who lived in slums, existed in unspeakable filth. Strangely enough, one compelling force that kept them in this condition of unsanitary effluvium was the edict of religious practice. It was held that the naked body should never be exposed; that to do so even for a bath, was a sin.

In the early days of contact, European ecclesiastics felt that, even though their bodies came out spanking clean, the Indians, by swimming in the lakes and flowing streams, were besmirching their souls. An example of this attitude can be read in the *Code of Burgos*, drawn up in 1512 in Spain—a directive purportedly designed to help Indians find "the way". Priests were instructed to "teach them their prayers in Latin and restrict their heathenish custom of taking baths." It is also, interesting to reflect on the fact that, even in the last days of the 19th century, there remained on the statutes of the City of Boston, laws to the effect that citizens were forbidden to, "immerse the entire body in water without a doctor's prescription."

Sanity however, finally prevailed. Indian souls appeared to withstand the danger of daily ablutions. And there were still further lessons to learn concerning the stimulation of blood circulation and purging through the skin. As Fraser Symington observes: "small, domed, sweat-houses could be seen at every more or less permanent campsite between Newfoundland and the Coast Range and somewhat less frequently on the West Coast itself." These structures held important religious and social meaning. They were utilized for easing aching muscles and for treating stomach cramps, respiratory disorders and other physical maladies. But more important, sweat lodges served as religious temples for cleansing the spirit.

The skeptical new arrivals observed such practices for many years, and gradually adapted to the concept of personal cleanliness through bathing. But there were some lessons to learn in the selection of appropriate clothing, particularly for use in the colder climates. Back in 1644, when the French adventurers paced their barricaded platforms at Montreal, they had been flabbergasted to see scantily-clad Iroquois scouts cavorting in the snowbanks and all in robust health. In later years, when Verendrye visited the Mandans, he was astonished to find that they did not even wear caps or mittens. The concept of wearing light-weight, insulating clothes as opposed to the heavy-matted fabrics started to catch on, and has increased even to the present generations. The idea of sleeping in the open air, or causing fresh air to circulate freely in sleeping quarters, is certainly of Indian origin. Modern man has invented air conditioners and heat exchangers today, but at one time, he did not know that this was the direction to go.

The Seek-and-Ye-Shall Find Formula

It is just simple logic to assume that intelligent human beings, detached though they were from the Eurasian mainstream, and living close to nature for several thousands of years, would make discoveries independently, and some completely unknown to their human counterparts in the rest of the world. The plant life is often different, yielding other medicines and other cures, but the process of trial and error has a universal application. People who observe nature and nature's processes closely had to come up with rewarding answers. Bones got broken and had to be set; people became mentally disturbed and had to be treated; some plants, taken into the digestive system, provided nutrients, others weakened the system and caused illness, while others cured illness and fought disease. Long years of close observation taught the Native People to identify and find applications. Many Indian women knew the cosmetic value of oils and plant juices when applied to the skin. Tribes of the Northern Woodlands knew the absorptive qualities of sphagnum moss. They used it for sanitary pads, general packing, and from it fashioned the first disposable diapers in Canada. These uses were not taken seriously by the newcomers until World War 1, when it was found that cotton wadding was not doing the job at front-line hospitals. A factory in Montreal, employing mostly Indian women, began to make surgical dressings from sphagnum moss which proved far more functional than cotton. Tests showed that while cotton pads absorbed six times their weight in water, sphagnum pads absorbed about twenty times their weight and three times faster.[6]

Bone setting was an Indian specialty. Their methods of applying splints utilized everything from strips of cedar to the flat, elastic ribs of cactus plants. Curves were filled out with wet clay, rawhide or moss. When anaesthetics were needed, to make bearable the pain of repairing wounds, amputations and removal of tumours, such narcotics as *datura* (jimson weed), *mescal* (peyote), and *cocaine* (from coca leaves) were used (cocaine is a modern derivative). In many cases, operations were performed by the use of sharpened agate scalpels, while boiling water was deemed necessary long before the practice was general in Europe, although the germ theory was unknown anywhere.

In other regions, Indian practitioners had been observed attaching an air sac (made from the bladder of small animals) to a hollow reed or bone, to be used as a syringe. There is some dispute in the matter of chronology, but some researchers declare that the Indians scored another first in this field.

The range of practice extended from the simple pulling of teeth to removal of poisoned arrow points and assistance at childbirth. Possibly, the most complicated surgery known was trepanning. Indians of the Andean areas of South America are known to have performed these operations, but

[6]Smithsonian Annual Report, 1918

skulls have been exhumed in the United States territory and in Canada, which also bear the marks of the art. Circular sections of bone were removed from the skull for the purpose of relieving pressure on the brain by removing tumours; we know that the patients survived because most skulls reclaimed show later bone growth sealing the point of removal. In the case of arrow wounds, the first action was to suck the wound clean and then apply various herbal juices. Slippery elm was often used to ease the offending foreign body to the surface.

Now, let us consider the subject of mental health and psychotherapy. Of course, the Indian practitioner did not call himself a psychiatrist, nor use such impressive terms as transactional analysis, behavioural therapy, or Freudian psychoanalysis, but he did have some basic understanding of phobias, tensions and the crippling effects of fear that cause people to have mental aberrations. He also knew how to apply the therapy of group participation and positive contactual thinking. By way of illustration, let us consider two random examples.

The medicine man in attendance at the side of the ailing one, might seek to put his or her mind at ease by pretending to suck something from the stricken body. Possibly a grotesque insect or other unidentifiable object would be displayed as the cause of the trouble. This, of course, is now recognized as a form of the placebo treatment.

Or, we may consider a recent development—a peyote ceremony, at the bedside of the sick. The well-wishers might gather about the patient, and during the hallucinatory experience, imagine that their immaterial minds would vacate their bodies momentarily and mingle with the sick man's immaterial mind, thus reinforcing it and changing its direction of drift toward the condition of recovery. And what is this, if it is not group therapy in action?

We are told today that many cases of mental disorders are caused by feelings of rejection. In all of these ceremonies, the prime objective was to affect a reunion of all forces of the body, mind and nature. Feelings of rejection are dissipated by establishing the patient firmly in his environment. In recent years, medicine men have been employed at various United States reserves, notably the Navaho, to use the traditional methods in treating mental and emotional problems. Jean Goodwill, a special adviser to the Ministry of National Health and Welfare in Canada, reported that in the prairie provinces, considerable success has been accomplished by using traditional methods to treat illnesses of a psychiatric nature (especially those where alcohol is a factor). In his book *Indian Healing*, psychiatrist-anthropologist Wolfgang Jilek documents the success of shamanic ceremonialism in the Pacific Northwest today.[7] It would appear that further acculturation in this field might be of mutual benefit.

The High Cost of the "We-Knew-It-First" Syndrome

Gynecology, obstetrics and pediatrics are impressive terms but, to the Indian women, they all meant the science of having a baby. To her, childbirth was a function of nature. Her European sister however, was plagued for centuries with the bugaboo of "original sin"—the notion that pain and discomfort was in some way a penalty to be paid for the moral indiscretions of Adam and Eve.

It is not surprising, therefore, to learn that Indian birthing methods used on this continent at the time of Champlain, were generally more advanced than they were in Europe. Dr. George Engelmann, in 1883, describing certain massage and manipulative techniques to expel the fetus, has written: "These methods have been recently rediscovered by learned men, clothed in scientific principle, and given to the world as new." The ease of childbirth and control of postpartum hemorrhage among native women, has long been a source of amazement to white observers. Then, seemingly to emphasize what Engelmann had said in 1883, Dr. Eric Stone, a prolific writer on Indian Medicine in the middle 1900's followed up with this statement: "Crede's method of expulsion was universally applied by the American Indian generations before it was described by the eminent French obstetrician."[8]

Dr. Stone singled out the Iroquois for special mention in his discussion of the Crede method, but of course, the same circumstances did not prevail in

---

[7]*Hancock, 1982.*

[8]*Medicine Among the American Indians* —Hafner Publishing Co. 1962

every environment. Melvin R. Gilmore, writing about the Arikara tribe in North Dakota (a 1930 paper) explains how, in case of malposition in the womb, the Arikara helpers "lift the woman and gently manipulated from the outside to change the child's position." Douglas Leechman, describing birth among the Vanta Kutchin in the northern Yukon, starts with the expectant mother sitting on the floor on a caribou skin. One woman sits in front, holding up her arms while a second assistant sits behind her for support and to supervise delivery. The umbilical cord is cut and tied with caribou tissue and the placenta is burned. The child is then placed in a bag of warmed loose caribou hair. Infants, among such bush tribes as the Ojibway, were kept washed with wads of reindeer moss that had been sanitized in boiling water. To repeat, there was an infinity of variations.

Birth control methods, too, were varied and widespread. Some Indians were aware of the "safe period". Among the Shoshone, Comanche and tribes of the Nevada area, women made a tea containing *Lithospermum*, using it as an oral contraceptive. Others used a powdered decoction of Indian turnip, or the rhizome and root of wild ginger, or an infusion of pulverized roots of milkweed. We know that the Iroquois women seldom had more than four children, so how was this accomplished? Even in modern times, anthropologists like Nicole Maxwell have come back from trips into the upper reaches of the Amazon and told us of the hundreds of contraceptive plants and fungi that are still used, and have been used for centuries. These many birth control devices, as well as prolonged nursing, were known to Indian women long before the advent of "the pill".

Women of the Blackfoot nation used the roots of prairie crocus to speed up labour pains. Ojibway healers prescribed the roots of Canadian violet made into a tea for bladder problems. Iroquois herbal uses leaned heavily on hemlock tea to eliminate scurvy. Hopi women used a decoction of Indian paintbrush to stop up menstrual flow. There seems to be no end to the information that has already been garnered for books. But as author Virgil J. Vogel writes in his excellent, five-hundred page volume, *American Indian Medicine:* "Just as America was considered to be undiscovered before the white man found it, so the Indian drugs were unreal or of no account until the white men discovered them". This is called ethnocentric bias.

So, it is with this thought in mind that we would continue to relate further information of general medical interest.

The cause of internal disorder, to the Indian mind, was linked with the total concept of order in the universe. It is true that the wonders of microscopic discovery had not yet been revealed to them, and therefore, the existence of viruses, germs and bacteria was totally unknown. But a deep-seated oneness with nature told them intuitively that if forces destructive to their physical well-being existed, there must also be curative forces to counteract them.

This form of spirituality, as we have already observed, encouraged the practice of external personal hygiene. It is also extended to the concept of internal purging. The impurities that accumulate in the digestive tract, it was thought, should be expelled through the mouth and rectum. The Iroquois, for example, used at least twelve different emetics, a popular vegetable derivitive, *Spiraea Ipecacuanha*, being one of them. Other tribes used spurge, dogbane, horse gentian and the various forms of ipecac, in South America. The Montagnais used steeped twigs from Canadian balsam fir to make a strong laxative. Other cathartics widely used were *cascara sagrada* (now available in bottles), *podophyllum* (May apple root), *jalap* (from a tuberous root), and *mechoacan* (sometimes referred to as the rhubarb of the Indians), were used in Mexico.

There were also preparations to stop diarrhea. The Hurons are known to have boiled cedar leaves; the Miamis brewed sumach leaves; the Delaware used Jack-in-the-Pulpit; the Oneidas used blackberry root; in Mexico many tribes used extracts of agave leaves; others used wild geranium, bayberries, hemlock and persimmon. And as a vermifuge (to remove worms) such preparations as the pulverized roots of pinkroot were used.

Burns, scalds, flesh wounds, abrasions and contusions were everpresent annoyances and a marked danger when ignored. So, for such external problems the native materia medica accumulated a long list. Plants of the mint family, for example, provided relief from insect bites. The Mohawks made a decoction from the bark and twigs of witch hazel to use as an astringent, and the stopping of blood flow. Burns were often treated with a strong decoction of tobacco. Ointments were made from seeds of jimson weed, buds of tulip trees, the boiled bark of basswood and a hundred and one other mixtures. Balsam was widely used as an antiseptic. The Chickasaws mixed alum with curative herbs as an astringent. By comparison with the crude medicine of Europe's "quacks" of the 1600's, says Fraser Symington in *The Canadian Indian*, "the Iroquois excelled in their treatment of wounds, fractures and dislocations, and their herbalists provided a great fund of knowledge to Europe."

Some of the treatments used seem almost bizarre in the modern context, but there are firm reasons to earn them merit. Many tribes found raccoon fat a wonderful antidote for sunburn. The Cherokee were known to have made plasters of buzzard down to stop hemorrhages. Indian snakebite remedies have not been proven to be effective. See*American Indian Medicine.* (pp. 220-24) Possibly the most remarkable treatment of all was the application of the spores and pulverized heads of certain species of puff-balls to stop bleeding and prevent infection used by such widely separated tribes as the Kwakiutls, Mohegans, Ojibway and Plains Indians. There are so many examples where the use of moulds, fungi and ashes were popular that it is not hard to surmise that many tribes had stumbled onto the healing qualities of penicillin or other antibiotics.

The Sellout to Frontier Falsification

We may ask what effect this accumulated knowledge of folk medicine had upon the arriving white men who came into early contact with the aboriginal people. Were they impressed? Did they take advantage of the various treatments?

In the initial stages, the answer would have to be "yes". Early settlers, landing in Quebec and on the Atlantic seaboard, had a rudimentary knowledge of European folk medicine but in a general way, they found Indian remedies more effective, more specific in use and more easily available. These first arrivals not only learned to prepare the medicines, but learned to use them in accordance with Indian custom. We read of the Pennsylvania Germans engaging in the spring rituals of "blood purification" with such medicines as sassafras, sarsaparilla, devil's bit and burdock. Many Indian women were in demand as midwives. Some methods of healing were written up in medical journals. Indeed, it can be said that Indian medicine enjoyed a reputation of respect among most frontiersmen.

But, as seems to be the general pattern with Western society, crass commercialism commenced to wreck the relationship. The possibility of exploiting aboriginal healing skills through cheap emotional appeal in the marketplace, was too much of a temptation for a growing host of charlatan promoters. Hundreds of nostrums were concocted and panned off on the public, purportedly as secret Indian cures, but fraudulently loaded with such useless ingredients as rum, molasses, sugar-water or alcohol. Such spurious concoctions as Kickapoo Indian Sagwa, Old Sachem Bitters, Wigwam Tonic, Seminole Cough Balsam and Comanche War Paint Ointment flooded the market, while an appropriate clutch of side-show vendors sprang up as a sales force. There were people like Texas Charlie, Nevada Ned and John Healy peddling nostrums such as Indian salve, cough cure and worm killer. During the 1880's, it is estimated that as many as 75 travelling Kickapoo shows toured the United States at one time. In New Jersey, a travelling spectacular made up of 100 performers mesmerized the yokels and sold up to 4,000 bottles a week of the Sagwa potion alone. It was not generally understood, but the trashy array of sugar-coated junk was seldom, if ever, of Indian origin, but rather the merchandise of unscrupulous white interlopers.

So in the melee of cheap chiseling, the prestige of Indian medicine took a slump and over the long term, the usefulness of Indian medicine to Western Society suffered a setback. Let us recount some of the knowledge that might have served mutual interests and provided a basis for earlier and more intense research.

In 1924-25 pharmaceutical historian, Herbert W. Youngken, compiled a list of 450 plant remedies used by the Indians. The Ojibway people, alone, accounted for 56 drugs which were found to have a specific medicinal effect and would have been of use to scientific researchers. Dr. Carl Koller used cocaine as an anaesthetic for the first time in 1884, but the Peruvian Indians had been using it for centuries. Quinine (an extract from cinchono bark) was known and used by South American Indians as a treatment for malaria. Indians of the coastal areas collected kelp as treatment for goitre, even though they didn't know there was such an element as iodine. Some tribes used a willow bark decoction to prepare a headache remedy; willow bark contains the salicin which is now produced synthetically as an ingredient of aspirin. For indigestion, the Papagos were known to boil red earth from under a fire, add salt and strain the liquid; this produced an antacid base, which counteracted stomach acidity—Tums for the tummy?

Toothache was almost unknown among the nomad hunters, but the corn planters, rice harvesters, maple syrup makers and some of the more sedentary tribes of the south required some dental attention. Many tribes chewed spruce gum to keep their teeth white, while the more southern types used the bark of prickly ash, as did the whites many years later. Curare, which was used to poison arrowheads, was also used as a medical stimulant or for shock treatment. Today it is used for convulsive therapy, as a nerve stimulant in anaesthesia and for treatment of poliomyelitis. An extract of foxglove was correctly used for its properties as a cardiac stimulator. It contained *digitalis*, which was "discovered" in England several hundred years later. And the list goes on—cohosh, puccoon, liquidambar, cochineal, genseng, etc..

Virgil J. Vogal, who has published one of the most complete records of Indian achievement in the curative arts under one cover, points to the lists that constitute the drug compendium used primarily by pharmacists today— *The Pharmacopeia of the U.S.A.* (dated from 1820) and *The National Formulary* (since 1888). He concludes that "The most important evidence of Indian influence on American medicine is seen in the fact that more than 200 indigenous drugs which were used by one or more Indian tribes have been official in these compendia for varying periods since the first editions appeared". And further, "In a surprising number of instances, moreover, the aboriginal uses of these drugs corresponds with those approved in *The Dispensatory of the United States*".

Of course, the listings do not direct the use of the drugs by the physician, and it is not contended that, in any case, the whites learned their uses from the Indians. What is indicated however, is that there has been an extensive exchange of ideas in both directions. Mutual acculturation is a form of therapy. Ethnic arrogance is a social disease.

Dr. Frederick Banting, Canadian discoverer of insulin, intended to write a book on native contributions to medicine, but was prevented by his untimely death. In it he wanted to give credit to North American Indians for doing the "pharmaceutical spadework", which led him to success. What a loss!

We wish to thank Dr. Virgil Vogel, for his reading and suggested corrections of Chapter Four, *The Gift of Better Health.*

5

CHAPTER

The Gift of Agriculture and Food

When Hernan Cortes and his retinue of Spanish soldiers entered the Aztec capital, Tenochtitlan (now Mexico City) they were bug-eyed with wonder at sights in the market place, both there and in the suburb Tlaltelolco. His chronicler Bernal Diaz, relates that "We stood amazed by the infinity of people and goods, and by the method and regularity of everything." An enormous space was given over to display of an infinite variety of goods. As well as precious stones, multi-coloured feathers, cotton fabrics, fur and rawhide, tables were laden with such items as cocoa, peppers, maize, beans, sweet potatoes, peccaries, turkey meat, agave, guava and many fruits they had never seen before. Women cooked maize cakes, tortillas and tamales on open-air stoves and utility items were stacked in neat arrangements everywhere. Cortes, himself, describes the scene by saying, "there is nothing like it in Spain."

When Jacques Cartier sailed into the Huron Village of Hochelaga in 1536, after passing interminable miles of forest, silent bays teeming with fish, and clumps of berry bushes hanging heavy with fruit, he was due for some further surprises. He was greeted by over a thousand friendly Indians bearing food. In his own account of the visit, he wrote: "It was a finer greeting than ever a father gave to his own child, and it made us marvellously happy. For the men danced in one band, the women in another, the children in another. And afterwards they brought us fish and the bread they make of coarse meal, throwing it into our ships in such quantities that it seemed to fall from the sky."[9]

[9]Basic Documents in Canadian History -James J. Talman

When the English colonists set foot on the tidewater shores of Virginia, the Pawhatans supplied them with new vegetables and sea food which sustained them well. "It pleased God", wrote Captain John Smith, "in our extremity, to move the Indians to bring us Corne, ere it was half ripe, to refresh us... great stores of Corne and bread ready made..."

Such expressions of interest in sustenance, coming from the lips of early European arrivals, seem somewhat exhuberant, but there was good reason for the interest. Not only were the newcomers hungry after a long voyage, but there was a lack of good nourishing food in their countries of origin.

In Europe, populations were increasing, internecine wars had become a way of life and agriculture had been sadly neglected. There was a limited number of field crops that had been brought to the state of sustainable yield and large areas of the Middle East were going to desert through overgrazing. Continuous leaching on the Iberian Peninsula and little knowledge of crop rotation anywhere left tracts of land semi-exhausted. Agriculture, in Eurasia, was in a bad state.

Records show that the average European male in those days was about five feet tall and his lifespan seldom went beyond thirty-five years. No wonder the new arrivals in Indian territory were somewhat awestruck!

Anyone who undertakes to make an inventory of all food commodities that have an origin in Indian agriculture, is confronted with the dilemma of deciding where to start. Since climate has so much influence on plant germination and growth, possibly the semi-tropical regions of this continent will yield the greater portion of plant species, so we will begin by looking at the tremendous accomplishments of the aboriginal peoples from what is now Mexico and Central America.

Aside from meat, the four staple foods of the Aztecs were corn, beans, amaranth and sage—and from these they made the many maize cakes and tamales. Of course, we know that the Tenochtitlan was built among a cluster of lakes where immense quantities of fish, caviar, frogs, crustaceans and certain other marine growth was harvested on a regular schedule. The entire complex was a maze of canals and waterways, while the drinking water was piped in from Chapultepec. Neat courtyards were maintained for community enjoyment, and everywhere flowers in profusion were nurtured for display. The urban dweller was a horticulturist of a very high order. His land allotment was under intensive cultivation and many backyards had their complement of gobbling domestic turkeys. The regular clipping of lawns would not be considered of any utilitarian value.

A unique method called the *Chinampa* system was used to produce phenomenal yields of grain and vegetables in the marshes. Rectangular shaped strips of land were formed by pushing up bottom soil and anchoring it around frames and posts to form what might be called floating islands. Canal water would surround each plot and new, rich soil would be scooped up from the marsh bottom to renew fertility. From this continuous revitalization, the land produced as many as six to seven crops per year.

The use of manure, compost and night soil was well understood and practiced throughout the entire area. Indeed, it is a tribute to the people's knowledge of control methods that such a dense population around Tecnochtitlan could live in a marshy environment without a threat of contamination. They were evidently able to maintain a balance between bacteria, insects, crustaceans, edible fungi and water succulents—not a simple task without the use of insecticides, fungicides and general chemical warfare.

The market place of the Aztecs was abundantly stocked with such utilitarian materials as dyes, cochineal, indigo, pottery, copper tools, a type of paper made from aloes, charcoal, flint, obsidian, bamboo pipes and various items of furniture made from woven reeds. And overseeing this operation were small groups of guardians whose sole function was to see that trading was fair, that those of a more predatory frame of mind did not cheat. Lacking any form of money system, they devised trading practices that were designed to affect equitable distribution rather than to make profit; thoughts of sharp practices were considered anti-social. But trading practice and agriculture are two different subjects, so let us not stray too far from the subject at hand.

In reviewing the entire array of foodstuffs brought into general use throughout Mesoamerica, we find that some success was attained in the domestication of animal species—turkeys, Muscovy ducks and even stingless honey bees. But by far the most socially significant triumphs were registered in the field of horticulture. Literally thousands of year before the arrival of Cortes, Indian agrobiologists had brought such plants as the tomato, squash, pumpkin, chili peppers, tobacco, cucurbits, cocoa (chocolate) avocado and as many as six varieties of beans into domestic production. But from the point of view of genetic manipulation and economic importance to mankind, the development of maize or Indian corn is a horticultural triumph which, in the words of Dr. Michael D. Coe has become "the most productive food plant on earth."

For more than a century now, white men have known that corn, in its present form, did not develop through a genetic evolution. It appeared to have no living progenitors; without the help of people it could not re-seed itself. Somewhere along its genetic journey, humans must have had a hand in its destiny. There was much theorizing in the ranks of modern archaeologists until in 1960, Dr. R. S. MacNeish and botanist, Dr. Paul C. Mangeldorf teamed up to discover and announce that small cobs, no larger than a cigarette filter, had been found in a cave and that there was a link between them and a wide-leafed grass that grew in the Tehucan Valley of Mexico. But what was the nature of this link? What plants were the progenitors? When the mystery was finally unravelled, all evidence pointed to this explanation.

It would appear that about the period 5000-3500 B.C., a small cornlike plant did indeed grow in the Tehuacan Valley. It was an insignificant grass plant with long plumes reaching up from pods carrying hard seeds resembling popcorn. Two protecting husks parted at the top so that seeds could be scattered by wind and birds. This plant together with beans, amaranth, chili, rabbits, birds, turtles, etc., helped feed the ancient societies that had settled in this sheltered zone. But in subsequent years the population exploded to about ten times its original size and a period of domestication of plants was given a new thrust. A tall grass called *tripsacum* which grew wild throughout Mesoamerica, was crossed with this early, open-faced seed plant and a hybrid called *teosinte* resulted.

By 3,000 B.C., according to G.H.S. Bushnell in *The First Americans*, about 30 percent of the plant life consumed by the Olmecs was from cultivated species, and maize was rapidly becoming a food staple because of the increased size of the cobs brought about by selective breeding and back-crossing. It is interesting to note that the original pod corn plant became extinct about 250 A.D., but the cross breeding of *teosinte* continued until the enlarged cobs became a dietary mainstay of those great civilizations known as the Aztecs, Toltecs, Teotihaucanos, Zapotecs, Mixtecs and Maya.

By the time Cortes arrived on the scene, corn had been established as a food staple, not only in Mesoamerica, but as far south as Peru and as far north as Ontario. Europe was hungry, so right from the start, shipments of this and other Indian domesticated foodstuffs started to move across the Atlantic to meet the needs of an impoverished Europe. Squash, green beans, peanuts, rhubarb and melons were among the early samples.

At the same time the Conquistadores, who had overrun the Pacific slopes of the Andes, had come in touch with another crop plant which was to become a nutritional bonanza for European tables. This edible tuber called *papas* by the Incas, had a history dating back to their predecessors, the Amaras, and beyond that stretching back about six thousand years. They now appeared in eight distinct species and were grown in over three thousand varieties. By the time they had been fully introduced to Europe, the name had been confused with a completely different tuber from Haite, which the Arawaks called *batatas* and they all became known as potatoes, sweet and otherwise.

Looking back now from the vantage point of spent history, it is interesting to note the social changes that occurred when the seed stock for all these new plants took root in European soil and began to multiply. The nutritional transfusion touched off a marked population explosion. For example, Ireland's human complement built up to a staggering eight million, more than double its present count. Holland, Germany, France and their neighbours also felt the surge. But the European agrobiologists had not planned well. They had gone overboard in dependence on too few varieties of potatoes before sufficient knowledge had been gained concerning the effects of humidity and disease control. By 1854, a deadly fungus blight struck the crop, resulting in famine and widespread misery.

During this period of distress however, experimentation continued both in North America and abroad, and the lowly spud responded to the new understanding. In Canada and the United States for example, modern agrobiologists have introduced twelve main varieties and the expansion has just begun. "New needs call for new breeds", as the saying goes. The Peruvian Indians in ancient times, had learned how to make a freeze-dried preparation called *chuno*, which could be stored for as long as four years. This inspired new ideas in dehydration. In 1853, a short-order cook named George Crum, is said to have invented and prepared potato chips at

Saratoga Springs, New York. Fittingly enough, he was an Indian. Present uses for the spud now include bread, flour, pasta, vodka and fuel for cars. As a world crop potatoes now rank fourth after wheat, corn and rice, but first in terms of energy and nutritional value per acre. Today, the world produces an average of 291 million tons annually, of which Europe and the Soviet Union grow 75% and the remainder is grown in the Americas and on the terraced mountainsides in such places as India and the Phillipines. Back in Lima where horticultural drama began, the International Potato Centre carries on scientific work designed to help solve a possible world food crisis in the 21st century.[10]

These have been the major contributions of the tropical and semi-tropical regions of the Americas. Now, let us move further north.

When the French gained entry to the continent through the Gulf of St. Lawrence, and the English established squatter's rights on the Atlantic seaboard, they were to be treated with further supplies for larders back home. Later, as the English penetrated further inland, the Lenni Lenape of the Delaware River country introduced them to bounteous gardens and some fruit orchards of note.

Further south, the Muskogean family of tribes were growing crops of millet, pumpkin, melons, sunflowers, corn and hickory nuts from which to make lye-hominy, persimmon bread and cornpone, foods the newcomers had never seen before and which remain popular to this day.

Deeper in the interior and further north, many tribes of the Algonquian family, inhabiting the maple forests, knew how to extract the sap from these hardwoods in the spring to make flavoursome maple syrup. Their Iroquoian neighbours in the Finger Lakes area below Lake Ontario, were agriculturists of a high order who grew corn in abundance for food and for trade. According to one authority, F.G. Speck, they raised from 15 to 17 varieties, one of which was a particular strain of popping corn. When dipped in maple syrup and allowed to harden, this became the famous "crackerjack" confection that had with variations, become popular in many lands to gladden the hearts of uncounted numbers of children.

[10]For reference see *NATIONAL GEOGRAPHIC Vol. 161 No. 5 May 1982 "The Incredible Potato"* By Robert E. Rhoades of this Centre.

The Iroquois also grew about 60 varieties of beans, 8 native squash plants, as well as harvesting 34 wild fruits, 11 nuts, 38 leaf and bark extracts, 12 edible roots and 6 useful fungi. They used a type of hoe to cultivate the soil (a sharp blade attached to a long handle) which took the eye of European garderners. What next? Well, it might surprise some Ontario residents to know that at the time Champlain contacted the Hurons and Petun tribes near Parry Sound, crops of corn, tobacco and sunflower were being grown as a major food to sustain the 30,000 or more local people and for trade to the more northern Ojibways, Nipissings and Cree. This present area, better known as Muskoka, is now considered more suitable for winter skiing and summer loafing.

In most parts of North America where the situation required it, some type of agriculture was practiced, but in the woodlands, on the prairie and along the coastal reaches, food was so plentiful that land cultivation seemed unnecessary. The gathering of wild rice by the Ojibway is a case in point. Every fall early in September, many of the marshy areas surrounding the Great Lakes were alive with canoes, parching racks and myriads of harvesters. One man poled the birch-bark canoe along through the shallow waters while his partner bent long stems of rice plants over the side, flailing and beating the seed-bearing heads onto a sheet of birch rind that covered most of the floor. A load of ten to twelve bushels, three times each day, was considered a good day's work, but that was only part of the process.

Women and children then took over and continued with the task of arranging parching racks under which fires kept an even heat to assure drying. Then came hours of husking and winnowing after which the grain was poured into containers for storage or trading. One branch of the Ojibway family called the grain *manohmin* and thus became known as the Menominees. To the Woodland Indians, wild rice was a grain staple which they used in many cooking combinations. On the shelves of twentieth century supermarkets, wild rice is usually found in the delicatessen section and is considered a gourmet's delight.

But this was just one annual crop. How about blueberries, wild raspberries, huckleberries, gooseberries and mushrooms? Since climates were more severe and the terrain more rugged, plant life was largely supplemented with the meat from big game. Chipewyans, Dogribs, Loucheau, Yellowknife, Kutchin and other tribes, who inhabit the short tree-belt called the taiga, followed the great caribou herds and knew their travel routes like a book. They also knew how to combine this meat with seasonings from crushed roots, species of moss and chosen herbs. Further south among the Kootenays and tribes of the Cordilleras, the protein mainstay was deer and other ungulates seasoned with wild onion, the roots of the tiger lily and certain tree mosses. The inside bark and gum from the larch made a stimulating drink and they did not overlook oregon grapes and rose hips as a nibbling delicacy. Today, we recognize both of these as a good source of vitamins.

But when it came to feeding on nature's bounty, the Indians of the Prairie Grasslands were particularly blessed. In the buffalo herds they had a moving chain of department stores, which delivered not only food, but clothing and shelter on the hoof. From the gigantic body of the animal they were able to obtain large quantities of meat for cooking and drying. Tongues were considered a delicacy and livers were rich in vitamin supplements. Tallow was added to dried and pulverized portions, flavoured with wild berries and stored as pemmican. Buffalo robes were made from the shaggy hides, ropes from rawhide strips, clothing and containers from belly hide and even tepee covers from the full-sized hides. Sinews were converted to webbing and bow strings and horns became drinking cups, eating utensils and buttons. For years after the great buffalo slaughter (which ended about 1875) both Indians and white frontier people depended heavily on "buffalo-chips" for fuel. In less violent days, these wandering herds had supplied most of the needs of Blackfoot, Cree, Assiniboine, Crow, Dakota, Pawnee, Cheyenne, Ponca and others for centuries.

On the Atlantic seaboard, Indians had taught the new arrivals how to gather kelp as a medicinal food and how to bake clams in heated sand on the beach. On the Pacific Coast, methods of fishing had developed to such a fine art, that many Europeans took note of the improvised gear and techniques. The Nootka taught them new methods of steaming fish, clams and mussels, while the Bella Coola boiled salmon roe, then added berries and sorrel leaves. Nobody anywhere has a monopoly on ingenuity.

Further south in the great drainage basin served by rivers running into San Franciso Bay, the many tribes of the Penutian family had found satisfactory methods to process nuts, bulbs and edible roots. Kouse, bitterroot, wild carrot, and carum were important, but the gathering and processing of camas bulbs and acorns provided flour from which they were able to make bread and cakes. The bitter tannic acid was leached out by a special process of washing after which the meal became edible.

Through a legacy from the Olmecs, Toltecs, and Maya Indians, our storehouses swell still further. Manioc (tapioca), pineapple, avocados (alligator pear), cassava, bananas, artichoke and peanuts are important items of diet today. Then, we can add domesticated strawberries, grapes, pecans, butternuts, sarsparilla, chocolate and various flavourings as an added treat.

Indian societies everywhere collected herbs, bark and roots for medicinal purposes and this has been treated more fully in another chapter of this book. However, some of the experimentation in this field has had spinoffs that now are becoming relative to agriculture.

Up until the present decade, it has been generally believed that control of insect pests in the fields and garden plots of America can be easily affected by the application of a new and improved array of insecticides; that the chemical industry can keep the growing host of creepy-crawlies at bay. But the battle still goes on, the varmints develop immunities and, worst of all, some of the chemicals are having a lethal effect upon the health of the very humans whom they were supposed to benefit. The banned list started with D.D.T., but is now stretched out to include captan, 2,4,5-D and a number of formula designations that add to the obscurantism of the control method.

Possibly a different approach at this time is indicated. Records show that some Indians gathered the roots of the coneflower, a member of the thistle family, to make a potion which was an antiseptic and an analgesic (pain killer). But this substance was also used to kill some insects and retard the growth of others. Even though this may not be the entire answer, possibly it points in the right direction; fighting nature's battles with nature's tools. It would seem that this is a type of field husbandry that deserves more current experimentation and attention. Possibly the white man still has something to learn from Indian methodology.

In totality the native American developed, grew and utilized such an array of grains, fruits and vegetables, that some agrobiologists of our time estimate that the aggregate now accounts for well over half of the world's agricultural wealth.[11]

[11] *The Indians of the Americas:* John Collier. p. 32. (Norton, 1947)

Indian societies were many in number and so were their accomplishments. No doubt there are many items that have been overlooked in this quick summation. Almost without exception, the knowledge and substance of aboriginal discovery has been given freely and without strings; their generosity was in the true Indian tradition of sharing. So, when we sit down next time to that fine Thanksgiving dinner—with its generous portions of roast turkey, mashed potatoes, cranberry sauce, green beans, corn-on-the-cob, pumpkin pie, and abundance of nuts and fruit—we should give a thought to the fact that we are eating an almost one hundred percent Indian meal.

This is what acculturation can do. But incidentally, how did the Pilgrims gain all the publicity? And how many of us give thanks where it is really due: to the North American Indian?

6

CHAPTER
The Influences of Folk Democracy

Good government may be described as the art of managing the affairs of numbers of people in a way that will bring about the greatest amount of internal harmony of the group, while at the same time fostering goodwill with neighbours. Politicians like to attach convenient labels to some particular form of control, but in the last analysis, the purpose (or motives) of the administration is the all important factor. Are the leaders really acting in the best interests of the people they seek to lead?

We look about us today and see confusion and distrust. We hear of scandals, mismanagement and chiselling in high places. Some factions talk of separation, there are charges of profit gouging through cartel collusion, a constant battle is waged to protect economic privilege and in some areas of Latin America, the violence of military rule seems so deeply rooted that decision-making is often an exercise in cruel, grinding repression. However, some forms of social administration have proven better than others, and that is what we want to consider here.

Has Western society learned anything through contact with the many Indian societies of North America?

If we were to put this question to many practitioners of the art of government today, few would concede that they have learned anything. Yet, history will tell us quite another story; indeed, it will tell us that this association has been a civilizing influence.

Before we can appreciate where we are however, we will gain a better perspective if we review where we have been. Only then can we know in what measure our behaviour patterns have been altered and in what direction.

Reviewing Ancestral Records

First, let us recognize that, in reviewing ancestral records, there seems to be a tendency to bask in the glory of victories and triumphs, while conveniently forgetting all the tragedies and shortcomings of the past. If we want to be objective, however, we must know that at the time of Columbus, Europe was solidly in the grip of the feudal system; that for the next three centuries, the people of Europe struggled to rid themselves of this type of bondage; and that even to the present day, remnants of this system remain to plague us. The constant bickering between labour and management, for example, can be recognized as a legacy of the servant-master relationship, and the inherent fascism of Latin America's military establishment is a persistent reminder of the Spanish conquistadores.

In feudal times, the landlord class ruled over a cringing, poverty-stricken peasantry. Child labour was an ever-present abomination. One of the more prevalent crimes was the theft of food and petty items of clothing, while the penalty for such misdemeanours was often imprisonment in rat-infested dungeons. Little wonder that sea-going ships were manned by the dregs of humanity who managed to escape this treatment. They were lucky to get away, to any fate.

In early times, all of Europe and Asia had been divided into tribal societies, as were the native people of the Americas. But for better or worse, their process of metamorphosis was different. At the time they began to reach out for more integrated trade and cultural exchanges with each other, they allowed themselves to become saddled by an upper class of master-trader whom they were expected to revere, obey and pay homage to at all times.[12] The acceptance of this code of class fealty was widespread; it permeated the national establishment, and as soon as water and land transport methods permitted a wider radius of mobility, it allowed the underlings to be used in all sorts of foreign conquests. Fifteen centuries of this conditioning produced a society which glorified conquest and struggle

---

[12]In contrast, it is interesting to note that the Aztec trading area, which extended over much of southern Mexico, also, had its regiments of commercial travellers known as the *pochtecha*. But these traders went about their work imbued with the idea of service and were not allowed to become haughty by accumulating personal wealth. See "The Daily Life of the Aztecs" -Souselle.

for power; it spawned a society which encouraged the exploitation of natural resources and used people as draft animals. Market values (expressed in terms of the price of gold) became so confused with real cultural values that some aspects of social behaviour approached a condition of psychosis. For example, when Cortes faked commiseration with Aztec emissaries after having first landed at Veracruz, he told them that his masters back in Spain were suffering from a disease that could only be cured with quantities of gold. His words were both prophetic and pathetic.

The idea of associating the concept of debt with the practice of trade was a feudal notion which no Indian society had ever considered. But in Europe, it became widespread and had a twofold effect; it created an involved accounting system for tabulating debt certificates, and it provided the traders with a tool by which favours could be bought and privileges maintained. The tabulators were called "bankers", the certificates of debt came to be known as "money", and the method has been named "price system". With this mechanism of leverage, conquests became more remunerative than negotiations and the decision-making process was largely vested in the hands of those who had the most direct access to total money supply.

While these centuries of conditioning were underway in Europe, however, the tribal societies of North America had gone an entirely different route. Indian leadership was both attained and retained on the basis of confidence and respect. An early visitor to the tribes of the Great Plains, Pierre de Smet, put it in these words: "If a chief does not succeed in gaining the love of his subjects, they will despise his authority, and quit him at the slightest opposition on his part; for the customs of the Indian admits no conditions by which they may enforce respect from their subjects." Function within the group came more from a desire to serve than having received a command. Without a price system, privilege could not be bought. The distribution of goods and services was more a function of rationing than the practice of buying and selling.

Another source of bewilderment to the Indian leadership in the days of early contact and a supplement to the money business, was the concept of "ownership", particularly as applied to land. What is "re-allocation"? Who "conveys title"? If "ecomienda" means that an Indian is part of the land and as such is attached as a slave, who made the rule? What is a "mortgage", or any other term of legal jargon, to people whose cultural background does not include price system methods of manipulation? It would be about as ridiculous to expect an Indian to comprehend the terms of some legal documents as a white Post Office employee to interpret the message inscribed on Ojibway birchbark scrolls, the records woven into Iroquois wampum belts or the hieroglyphic writing on the Mayan glyphs in Yucatan.

Another facet of Indian behavior was the complete tolerance of varying religious views both within the tribe and in neighbouring associations. Possibly some of the more intricately structured societies such as the Toltec, Aztec and Maya, leaned toward a more didactic manner. And few tribes followed the white man's concept of anthropomorphism (attributing human shapes and personality to a deity). The Indian perception of a god or gods was largely directed toward forces found in nature—to the wind, Mother Earth and above all, to the sun from which all life emanates.

And it was this fundamental precept of divinity or supreme intellect that set the two cultures apart; the one found it necessary to proselytize in order to bring converts to its particular personal theocentricity, while the other precept was based on phenomena of nature that were constantly observable. From the time Cortes arrived at Veracruz with his complement of spiritual advisors, to the days when frontier missionaries travelled the Saskatchewan prairie, North American history has been punctuated with strife, bewilderment, misunderstanding and martyrdom, because of the urge to convert. Possibly Red Jacket, a Seneca chief, expressed his sense of frustration best when he retorted after a scriptural session with an over-zealous proselyte: "Brother", he said, "If you white men murdered the Son of the Great Spirit, we Indians had nothing to do with it; it is none of our affair. If he had come among us, we would not have killed him; we would have treated him well. You must make amends for your crime yourselves."

This state of confusion has continued not only between Indians and white men, but between various Christian denominations themselves competing for converts. Indeed, on many Indian reserves in this twentieth century, the multiplicity of denominations acts as a divisive force while in the world arena, in such places as Iran and Ireland, the competition goes on and the acrimony which it breeds occasionally breaks out in military conflict.

Some Forms of Indian Decision-Making

Certainly it is not the purpose of this discourse to paint the Indian societies as models of perfection. They were not, and they were varied in their approach to social management. Systems of government ranged in complexity from loosely knit forms of hunting-gathering bands to the more involved confederations and city-states. Without getting too deeply into detail let us list a few. There were the Pueblo, Zuni and Hopi village-dwellers; unions such as the Powatan, Wappinger, Blackfoot and Iroquois tribal Confederacies; the totem clans of the Pacific Northwest; the Muskhogean and sun worshippers of the Gulf; or the simple Shoshone culture of the Great Basin. All of these groupings and many more, had widely differing forms of administration, but every society had a system which adapted in a considerable degree to the environment it occupied. The extent to which the administrative rubber band was stretched can be realized if, for example, we consider the variations within the Uto-Aztecan linguistic family alone; the complex Aztec society had a common origin with the simple desert dwellers sometimes referred to as the "Digger" Indians of Nevada, whose social organization did not extend much beyond the simple family unit. Yet the Aztec city-state was a highly integrated conglomerate.

And all of these group organizations had their strengths and their weaknesses; human sacrifice was practiced in some instances, self-mutilation in others, and a form of slavery is said to have taken place among groups such as the Aztecs, the Muskhogeans and tribes of the Pacific Northwest. Human sacrifice, we might point out, was a matter of religious practice (as was witch burning in Europe), self-mutilation was a matter of ritual (as was the attainment of sabre scars in Europe). But Indian "slavery" according to many anthropologists, was of a different nature than that practiced as an adjunct of Eurasian commercialism, so it needs more scrutiny here. Jacques Souselle, the French anthropologist, explains that slavery among the Aztecs was actually a form of benevolent welfare. Members of society who had mental or physical handicaps, often attached themselves to the more capable citizens in a form of voluntary service. People convicted of minor crimes were often required to serve the person they had wronged in a type of punitive servitude, thus eliminating the need for prisons.

Cortes, the Spaniard, dismantled the Aztec system of government and supplanted it with his own particular brand of organized terror. Decision-making to his mind, was a form of autocratic dictatorship under which internal order was inflicted by the sword, and which resulted in more Indians being sacrificed to the god of money than ever went to the sacrificial alters of Huitzilopochtli, main god of the Aztecs.

When the Spaniards ventured further into the interior of the continent, they were to see more forms of government which were new to them. Coronado and his minions arrived in Pueblo country in 1593 and found a far more democratic regime than they had ever known back in Spain. Unfortunately, they were too arrogant and too ignorant to recognize the fact. The word "Hopi" is a name these people gave to themselves. It means "the peaceful ones". The Spaniards reported an estimated population of up to 30,000 people living in 71 pueblos that stretched west to where five plazas and 16 kivas of Zuni shared space with them though they spoke two completely different languages. Surely this was an object lesson in democracy. According to William Brandon in *American Heritage Book of Indians*, some towns were divided into two birthright groups, each group taking its turn at town administration for a six month period. In other towns, the head of a particular society, chosen by its members, became the town leader as an automatic procedure. Of course we know that Coronado was not impressed but his records and reports carried the message.

The Creek Confederacy of the Lower Mississippi and the Pawnee Republic of the Central Plains were experimenting with more representative forms of decision-making long before the word "Republican" was used by the new arrivals.

The Algonquian Model

Further north, when the French and English began to penetrate to the home territory of the great Algonquian family, they found forms and ways which were destined to influence their future outlook. When tribes such as the Abnaki, Micmac, Delaware, Shawnee, Ojibway, Cree and others of their widespread family, were confronted with issues to be settled, they gathered in conclaves which would include women, children, medicine men and warriors, to hear the various points of view. Nobody had heard of women's suffrage, or secret ballots; issues were to be discussed and a consensus must be reached so that joint action would assure the best results. When the wider aspects of discussion had been dealt with and general decisions made, the council part of the conference ended and the smaller leadership groups met to plan details. This latter session was known as a *cau-cau-a-su* from which the English adopted the word "caucus".

The Algonquian way of arriving at consensus was not only democratic but had its roots in the very psyche of its people. Because they had no developed system of writing, memory retention had evolved to a remarkable degree. By associating ideas with objects so that events could spring to memory at the sight of tangible objects, they discovered that they had a natural adaptation that was both an art and a discipline. This artistry is evident in the generous use made of similes and metaphors as tools of oratory. The need for discipline is intrinsic to the entire process.

It is a fact that truth is essential to accurate verbal communication. When information is not recorded on paper for verification, the onus for factual presentation lies with the memory and honesty of the speaker alone. Credibility is of paramount importance. Of course, there was latitude allowed for fantasy, but deliberate lies were a type of tribal treason. Incredible though it may seem, these were the very attributes that later made it difficult for Indians to cope with the political chicanery and commercial propaganda of their new white associates. Native honesty was construed as naivete.

The Iroquois Tree of Peace

As we have observed with the Algonquian tribes, symbolism and government were closely aligned. This can be seen with even greater emphasis among the Iroquois. The Five Nations Confederacy was conceived as a Great Tree of Peace by its founder, the "Peace Maker", perhaps about the year 1450. He is said to have been born a Huron, but lived as an adopted Mohawk near the present site of Kingston, Ontario. Legend has it that he was of virgin birth. Whatever the facts, it is clear that he was a man of great mental stature, a philosopher who had keen insight into the art of human governance. When he stood before the first council of the Confederacy at

Onondaga, he pictured the tree as a protective symbol, its branches signifying shelter, the long white roots reaching out to the four quarters of the earth embracing any tribes or nations that would come in peace. At its summit perched an eagle signifying watchfulness. When these symbols were lodged in the people's minds by the chief orator, Hiawatha, they acted as the necessary glue to hold the Confederation together. And all this was happening at a time when Macchiavelism was coming to flower in Italy, Constantinople fell to the Ottoman Turks and Christians in Europe had just begun to condone usury (or adding interest on debt) as acceptable business practice.

The Longhouse People or Hotinonshonni, visualized a council of 50 peace chiefs sitting around five fires, one fire for each nation but all members of the same household. Within each nation the clan mothers appointed the sachems (peace chiefs), men who from childhood had shown wisdom, humility, and a willingness to serve others. The clan mothers continued to advise the sachems and could remove them from office for improper conduct or neglect of their responsibilities (although the normal tenure was for life). A second group of administrators or "pine-tree chiefs", gained position for some outstanding talent in a particular line of enterprise, and had the right to speak in all councils. Decisions were made by consensus, after a complex system of discussion. Each of the five nations—Mohawk, Seneca, Cayuga, Onondaga, and Oneida—was given special functions and designated territory to defend. The League was "rich in ideals that unify people in spite of their differences". As settlers pushed westward from the Atlantic, European weaponry tried to disperse the Confederacy. Still the Longhouse people spread their message of unity under the Tree of Peace. Overtures were made to the Hurons, Montagnais, Algonquins and even French colonists. When these groups refused to join the League, and continued to attack, the League retaliated. But many Indian nations did seek sanctuary with the League, yet were allowed to continue their own traditions (such as the Piscataways, Nanticokes, Dapinis, Tutelos, and the Tuscaroras who became the sixth "Nation").[13]

[13]Grinde, Donald. *The Iroquois and the Founding of the American Nation.* Indian Historical Press, 1977.

In attempting to understand the methods of administration used, there is one feature which appears to be greatly misunderstood even to this day. That is the use of wampum as an almost indispensible aid to smooth functional procedure. When immigrants come to any strange land it seems that they have a strong urge to label and view new phenomena in terms of what they find familiar at home. An equally erroneous idea is the concept that wampum should be associated in some way with what Europeans had come to know as money. Let us examine this ethnic blooper a little more thoroughly.

When coins were found to be of limited use to the trading fraternity of the Mediterranean and Arabian Sea areas, paper money was introduced as an experiment. Paper money had two interesting features as far as the feudal lords were concerned. It facilitated accounting in large volumes of goods: and as certificates of debt, could be manipulated as an instrument of social control over the debtor groups. Paper money, in all its forms, is nothing more than a "promise to pay", certificates of debt that carry or "earn" a rate of interest according to arbitrary rules. So what about wampum?

If we consult Webster's New World Dictionary, we can read that wampum is a short form for the Algonquian word *wampumeag*. Then it says, "small beads made of shells used by North American Indians as money, for ornaments, etc." Now, let us examine the function of wampum as it was used and in light of the definition of money given above.

In the beginning the concept of wampum belts had its roots in the symbolism adopted by the Iroquois Confederacy. Hiawatha is credited with having conceived the idea. In the law (or constitution) laid down by the founders, a belt of shells was woven to provide a stimulus to memory for each matter of concern. When addressing the Council each chief arose and held in his hand the relevant string of wampum. It served not only as an historic record upon which he could orient his discourse, but was an automatic check on fact and truthfulness. At the disposal of each item of business, wampum belts were hung on a horizontal pole in the council chambers. In this context, it is not difficult to understand why the belts were revered. They gave authenticity to mere words and fostered honesty in negotiations. In a sense, they were the Congressional Record or the Canadian Hansard.

When the League became operative as the Kanonsionne (Completed Cabin), a special official was selected as Keeper of the Wampum Belts. But, having succeeded with this consolidation, the League did not intend to remain static. It looked forward to a dynamic future in association with neighbouring societies and, as crusaders for a better world, they needed a method of recording dates and events. Meetings often included visiting dignitaries and, in later years, representatives of the English and French colonial powers. But always the procedure of meetings was the same.

When it came time for making inter-tribal treaties or lasting agreements, the wampum belts had an added function. It was like recording the terms of a contract in indelible ink. Belts of wampum, some several inches wide and in colours of white and purple, set down the terms and conditions in such a way that they could be easily referred to or memorized. Indeed, the repository of these belts was the national archives.

Of course, if we look at this truly Native innovation through the conditioned mind-set of European immigrants, it is understandable that they should look for some parallels. But where is the basic similarity between wampum which records facts and events, and "money" which merely assesses the "relative value" of everything but does not actually measure anything?

As contact increased, quantities of porcelain beads were arriving from Europe as trade goods. Beadwork decorations on moccasins, skin jackets and utility items became such an artistic challenge to the multitudes of Indian bands across the land that they gained a monetary value on the white man's open market. This development has reinforced the false belief that wampum was some form of "primitive" money.

The Acculturation Benefits

So, what happened to the Iroquois dream of peace? Was the time not yet ripe for such sensible idealism? At any rate, the people of the Longhouse left their mark on society and the remarkable thing about the entire administration is the fact that at no time did the Five Nations Confederacy have a population in excess of fifteen thousand men, women and children.[14]

[14]See: *White Roots of Peace* - Paul A. W. Wallace
(Akwesasne Notes, 1981)

But although the numbers were small, the social influences of Iroquois experimentation were tremendous. It would be difficult to look at the foregoing blueprint and not see glaring points of similarity to the form of administration adopted by the United States of America in its original constitution—with its association of independent states, its house of representatives and its senate of experienced statesmen. Nobody is suggesting that the U.S.A. stole the complete blueprint, but it is a well-known fact that the Iroquois Confederacy had a profound influence on the formation of the new regime. The United Nations was also based on an almost identical idealism. It might be noted that even today, when the United States gets into difficulties of a serious nature, it is usually because they have lost sight of the original motivation. And this all prompts us to pose a simple question: If ancient Greece can boast of its Aristotle and Plato, why should America not sing the praises of Hiawatha and the Peace Maker?

Possibly the Indian concept for mutual welfare, brotherhood and the need for public participation did not take root at once, but the delayed action continued to filter through. People who believed in "manifest destiny" and "the divine right of kings" would not change behaviour patterns overnight. The folk democracies of the North American Indians not only influenced the form of national governments on this continent, but these influences were carried to the very doorstep of the feudal societies themselves in Europe.

As early as 1575, the French essayist Michel de Montaigne, criticizing social institutions at home, drew a hypothetical picture of an Indian looking at the squalid scene in Paris "with half the people enjoying all the comforts, while the other half is begging in the streets in front of their doors." He suggested that the Indian would not "be able to understand why this disadvantaged half would not kill the other half and burn their houses."

By the time the French Revolution was underway, many writers of the day had versed themselves in the merits of the Indian classless societies, and there is little doubt that the pens of Rousseau and Voltaire developed a special zest when drawing parallels between the plight of the suffering peasants of France and the hypothetical man of nature they sought to describe.

Gertrude Hafner, a German academic, wrote a historical analysis of the influences of Indian social forms on the rise of socialism in Europe. Such political theorists as Engels and Marx often looked to Indian societies for evidence to support their particular analysis of class struggle.

Many political pundits have pondered the parallels that exist, comparing traditional Indian practice and European political theory, but they all miss the main point. Like the white man's erroneous concept of the function of wampum, the basic social principle which sets the Indian way apart, is misunderstood. Traditional Indian trading practices are different. The Indian rejects the notion that the debt certificates are necessary as an instrument of accounting. Putting it another way, the Indian mind is not concerned with whether an individual's politics lean to the left or the right. He knows intuitively that so long as the monetary structure functions to bestow privilege to either left or right, it misses the social criteria of equitable sharing that is his traditional birthright as an Indian. He uses the money system because he has to. But it does not fit with his heritage.

Although American and Canadian society clings tenaciously to ways of the Old World and in a sense is a reflection of European institutionalism, it would be wrong to say that Indian folk-democracy has not been a modifying and tempering influence. During the seventeenth century for example, a Delaware chief so impressed the local Democratic Party in New York State, that his name was adopted together with an officialdom of sachems and sagamores as a symbol of prestige to drum up voter strength. We are told that this pseudo-Indian organization, known as the Tammany Society, enjoyed initial successes, but later deteriorated into a political machine of rather questionable worth. Why? Because it was used to buy favours.

Other influences fortunately, have been more logically conceived and thus more durable. The meetings of fraternal societies for the purpose of mutual community help, are Indian in nature, and they often use Indian symbolism to mark their identity. We can compare the generosity of Indian tribal societies toward their less fortunate neighbours with the "foreign aid" tradition of Canada and the United States.

Over the past century in North America, there has been a gradual social transition toward religious tolerance. The ecumenical movement within the churches is a good omen. Rules for employing workers now forbid discrimination on the basis of religious affiliation. Political positions are held by adherents to a wider spectrum of denominations. Vast numbers of the general public do not affiliate themselves with any organized religion.

Possibly like the Indians, they see enough in the wonders of the world about them to be comfortable with the challenge of keeping in unison with the nature-plan as directed by the Great Mystery.

Now as the twentieth century draws to a close, when alternate energy sources have to be tapped as petroleum resources dwindle, when our forests require husbandry and some mineral deposits are on the short-supply list, the industrial minds, crystalized in the traditional mind-set of feverish exploitation, appear to be approaching some sort of ecological impasse. Businessmen say that exponential growth is the foundation of the Western way of life. Some environmentalists declare that a fundamental about-turn in thinking may be necessary for mass survival. Be this as it may, a wide segment of North American society is coming to the conclusion (consciously or otherwise) that the Indian attitude toward the environment is more valid now than it has ever been. Much of the writings supporting the "ecology movement" decry the mistreatment of Mother Earth.

Intellectual theorist, Alvin Toffler, author of *Future Shock*[15] warning of the perils of tomorrow, does not suggest a method that will eliminate the concept of unbridled commercialism. But he does speak almost wistfully of something called "participatory democracy". One wonders if this particular brand might not resemble the ideas envisioned by the Peace Maker more than five hundred years ago—or Red Cloud, Crowfoot, Tecumseh, Handsome Lake and many of their successors? Many Indian leaders in the modern context have important things to say, if anyone is listening.

[15]Bantam

7

CHAPTER

A Vision Experience for Tomorrow

After four hundred years of benevolence on the part of America's Native People, it might be expected that by this time, everything of value would be sapped from their stores of experience. In foregoing chapters, attention has been focused upon the more tangible contributions to our lifestyle in the fields of agriculture, language, sports, health, medicine, survival techniques and folk democracy. But acculturation is an ongoing process, and the end has not yet come. Is it possible that entering the twenty-first century, we are now approaching another crucial juncture in our journey together, when the greatest gift of all can be to our mutual benefit, if only we have the wit and the analytical capacity to understand and adjust?

Let us examine the essence of Indian religion.

Thirty years ago, to mention the term "vision seeking" in reference to the spiritual side of Indian life, would be to conjure up thoughts about manipulation of symbols, mystic aspects of a peyote session, or simply the visitation of dreams in a wilderness retreat. As we have seen, the religious rituals of the various tribal societies differed greatly. They were also interpreted from many differing points of view.

Social anthropologists investigating Indian folkways spent untold hours cataloguing and labelling all of the manifestations and tribal variations. And because many of these investigators were working in an academic haze and were so imbued with discovering differences, they neglected to emphasize the significant spirituality permeating all Native thought.

However, times are changing. Today we are starting to pay attention to the central theme that is subtly threaded throughout the entire spectrum of Indian ritual—the essential assumption that God is not merely a personality, but that all natural laws, forces and manifestations of this universe are both Creation and Creator. As one writer observes: "their passion for earth and its web of life transcends anything we have seen in other societies."

How can we explain a taboo which prevents the Micmac hunter from throwing the bones of a beaver back into the lake after having consumed its flesh, if we do not recognize a bond of common interest with the living beavers who still inhabit that lake? How do you explain the sacramental burning of sweetgrass, if you do not perceive a spiritual union of the worshipper with this particular member of the plant world through the fragrance of the smoke? Too often these concepts have been frowned upon as primitive "paganism" (whatever that means).

With growing concern for problems in our environment however, the subject of Indian spirituality is attracting wider and deeper interest. The realities of resource depletion are disturbing, but they often translate as the moral weaknesses of greed while the ongoing search for energy supplies is convincing a growing number of people in the "white" society that industrial attacks on nature do indeed have spiritual implications.

Twenty years ago, to suggest that the building of dams, bridges, thoroughfares and pipelines across environmentally sensitive areas might be courting disaster, or that the dumping of wastes in hidden-away-places could be anti-social, might sound ridiculous. Any adjustment to the natural topography would receive the official stamp of approval so long as it carried the magic label of "development" and was purportedly destined to create jobs. Today this thesis is being questioned. Hurricanes create jobs; houses of prostitution create jobs; wars create jobs; but what of the social consequences of this employment? What would be the aftermath of an oil spill below the ice in the Arctic? What has been the social cost of acid rain on the fish stocks of Ontario?

This is a basic transition taking place in thinking patterns, and it is nothing more than a slow movement toward the religious concepts that held sway in this land area for many thousands of years before the arrival of Columbus. It is nothing less than a vision experience we must necessarily feel if we wish to win the favour of the Great Mystery in assuring human survival.

So we ask: What is the theme of this spirituality that is so basic to all Native religious thought? Can we define its precepts?

Some Voices of Reaffirmation

Dr. Art Blue, an Athapascan Indian, who lectures at Brandon University in the province of Manitoba, has placed the entire idea in capsule form with the use of the Slave word (pronounced, Slavey) *de onde a da* which means "how things go together". The Indian, Dr. Blue explains, conceives not one world, but four worlds co-existing together. They are the physical world, the plant world, the animal world and the world of man—and in that order of importance. Of these "man" is the most insignificant because his very existence depends entirely on the other three. They can exist very well without him, but if any one of the other three were to be withdrawn man would perish. Life is a process of accommodation within a defined cycle of nature and it is man's job to adjust to the other worlds in order to gain the best rewards. That is the only way he can understand a "Creator".

A reading of many Native publications today—both Native-authored books and Native newspapers—will reveal that these concepts have not been forgotten. They bespeak a continuity of life which reaches back into antiquity. No matter how many millenia people have existed on this earth, its last generation is a link with the past and because of this immortality, all present living members have a responsibility to the generations that are to come.

All members of the great Algonkian family, for example, conceived a kind of brotherhood between man, animal, birds and plants—all guarded by a supernatural power. Each person had a guardian spirit or totem—upon which he could call in times of difficulty. The word "totem" itself comes from an Ojibway word *ototeman* which roughly translates as "he is my relative". Such a bond with a fellow living creature was the matrix which made this man of the forest a living part of his environment. His god was not a remote concept, but a living force whose presence could be felt in the wind, smelt in the forest or heard in the distant roll of thunder.

With these experiences of a Great Mystery it would be difficult for Indians to conceive of humans having souls, while other living creatures were denied such an important spiritual faculty. Mother Earth gave birth to all creatures and kinship was vital. It was inconceivable that humans should be divinely ordained to rule the earth. That was the role of the Great Mystery in accordance with certain immutable laws that had been set down as guidelines. Betray them at your peril, defy them and your place will shortly be taken by a more deserving successor.

The lodestar to human behavior was a reverence for the sacred harmony that could be observed in nature. Every act of existence—eating, breathing, sleeping and making love—is an act of regeneration. People live and die in a sacred manner, and if some animals and plants must die in order for humans to live, they must be taken with reverence, respect and gratitude.

Vine Deloria Jr., a student of comparative theology and an articulate writer from the great Sioux Nation, discusses the subject of creation in his book *God is Red*. He points out the basic differences between the Native religions and those of Europe: that one perceives the world in terms of time, and the other in terms of space. For the European, creation happened "then" but for the Native People, creation is happening "here" and "now". "Indian tribal religion," he explains, "could be said to consider creation as an ecosystem present in a definable place".

Traditionally Indians are keen observers. Traditionally too, they are reticent to speak their inner feelings because they have been taught that it is impolite to offend the feelings of another human being. But sometimes the sacrilege they see cannot be endured in silence. Max Gros-Louis, Chief of the Hurons, protests in his book that "to Indians, the real "savages" are those rapacious men with no morality who act only for profit, denying any disinterested friendship." Of the development tycoon whom he met in the Quebec woods, this Huron has these harsh words to say: "He absurdly claims that he is civilized simply because thanks to his looting, he has managed to become richer." In conclusion, Max Gros-Louis declares that, "To the native Indians, civilization does not consist of huge treeless cities inhabited by robots who have no communication with nature."

No, indeed! Communication with nature is important to the Indian—and it is important to his white brother as well, whether or not he knows it. The white man is subconsciously drawn to the wilderness areas to discover his origins. Even in the exhaust fumes of city traffic, he is impelled to go on camping trips and weekend visits to the backwoods "to get away from it all". The Appalachian Trail in the United States and the Bruce Hiking Trail in Ontario are both living testimony to this need. City dwellers paint bird pictures on restaurant place-mats, scenery on shopping bags, flowers on toilet tissue and even forget-me-nots on the bags used for emergency situations on jet airliners. He tries to forget, but he cannot escape—because he wants and needs solitude in order to understand himself.

So what is going wrong with the white man's world? Why has it come to a state when he must send his huge earth-moving machinery into the wilderness to rip the cover from the earth, to lay pipelines, to disrupt the quiet of the forest with the ever-increasing chatter of chainsaws, to poison water systems with the effluent of more and more papermills and to leave lethal doses of mercury to cause poisoned fish and a health hazard to people who must eat them? Would it not be timely to ask why we need more paper mills? More coal mines? Must we add to the flow of traffic on crowded highways while we search frantically for more energy sources to propel it? Do we need to continue mining more uranium ore in order to make our lives more radioactive? When will "progress" finish "progressing?"

A New Century - A New Dilemma

That last question may sound strange but it serves to point up the greatest dilemma of our time. It poses a paradox; it couches a contradiction; and it underlines the feeling of utter confusion that overshadows the economic life of all inhabitants of this great continent.

About three hundred years ago when Europeans began to flock to America in growing numbers, they found a fertile, sprawling land-mass bountifully endowed with resources. Here were eight million square miles of territory, stretching from the arctic to the tropics, affording the greatest variety of climatic conditions for the growth of vegetation. The internal network of lakes and rivers constituted a reservoir for storage of fresh water on a scale unknown to other continents, and subterranean reaches and rock outcroppings held a lion's share of the world's mineral deposits, together with generous quantities of coal, petroleum, natural gas and a wide spectrum of chemicals.

To this earthly treasure came the Western Europeans with their cultures of the Occident—a many-sided conglomorate of concepts gleaned and assembled from earlier cultures that for thousands of years had moved, mingled, acted and interacted along the Mediterranean trade routes, venturing forth in all directions in search of new lands and distant frontiers.

But their concept of the natural world was completely different from the precepts just described as the foundation of Indian spirituality on this continent of North America. The marauding Latins, Anglo-Saxons, Slavs, Norsemen, and Dutch had no such feelings of affinity toward their environment. Indeed, the system of economic control, which we have already described as the price system, was essentially geared to the exploitation of resources held in nature and at as great a speed as technically possible. This conviction too, was spurred on by a religious doctrine that placed man at the top of the hierarchy—holding dominion over all living things.

Now, let us see how he has applied this credo.

Since the first days when European businessmen arrived on the North American shore, they started forming corporations, and a tremendous industrial mechanism was in the making. With a never-ending flow of ingenuity and enterprise on their part, with the supine acquiescence of the academic and engineering fraternities, and the willing help of labour for wages, they have built and forged the greatest array of technological apparatus of all time—a veritable powerhouse, largely driven by the extraneous energy found stored about in random deposits of the fossil fuels we have come to know as coal and petroleum.

But with the approach of the twenty-first century, something has gone radically wrong with the dream.

On the one hand, the cry has gone up of an impending energy crisis, brought about by the diminishing supplies of these fossil fuel reserves—a crisis that could threaten to bring much of the great juggernaut to a grinding halt with its attendants, unemployment and financial distress. On the other hand, the vast industrial complex of America lies brooding in the valleys, along the lakefronts and in the harbour areas converting the remaining coal and gas supplies to sulphurous compounds that are carried on the winds and find their way to the wilderness areas to stunt vegetation and ruin the habitat of fish. Faced with a public outcry concerning the effects of acid rain, some elements of the business world have grasped in desperation at the nuclear option, preferring to take their chances with radiation damage. But others see in nuclear development a threat to the very existence of man.

So where must we turn for answers to this dilemma?

If there is one field of endeavour in which the proponents of Western culture have specialized and become proficient, everyone will have to concede that it is the study of scientific methodology and its application. Technologists and engineers are taught to confirm the logic of their actions by tools of measurement. Yet, to take even a cursory glance at some of these measurements gives us cause to wonder whether or not these scientists have looked at their own data lately, or whether they have just abrogated all reason and responsibility over to a clutch of their corporate masters.

A quick examination will prove illuminating.

According to a 1972 Review of Energy Resources, published in 1974 by the U.S. Geological Survey, life-giving energy from the sun has been received on Mother Earth for untold ages. To conceive of the amount is almost incomprehensible to the human mind. We know that much of the energy which comes from the sun is reflected back into space, but geophysicists estimate that approximately 122,000 times 10^{12} watts (that is, 122,000 multiplied by ten to the 12th power) is the fraction that is responsible for the earth's climate and principle material circulations. About 47% of this (82,000 ^{4} 10^{12} watts) is absorbed into the water systems and land blocks as heat. Another 23% (40 x 10^{12} watts) is captured by the green leaves of plants and provides the life force for growth.

Since the average rate of energy released by oxidation is almost exactly equal to the rate of storage, the total stock of living matter on earth remains relatively constant. But, from time to time over the years, very small fractions of plant and animal materials have become deposited in peat bogs and other places where oxidation is slow. Deposits such as these have accumulated during the past hundred million years or so. These miniscule amounts of stored energy are what now constitute the coal deposits, oil shale, tar sands, and pools of liquid petroleum we speak of as fossil fuels. Quantities are finite and, because of the amount of waste given off in combustion, they constitute one of the "dirtiest" forms of energy.

An impartial observer looking at the "energy crisis" from a neutral position might naturally ask the question: "Where is the problem? So the fossil fuels are nearing exhaustion. They were dirty, polluting and unhealthy. Good riddance! Particularly when the sun continues to shed its radiance and strength on this globe and this can be collected through plant growth, waterfalls, tides, wind and direct radiation—all known as the solar option.

Where is the 'crisis'?"

The only valid answer can be found by examining the basic operating characteristics of the price system itself. We have observed in an earlier chapter, that the system of monetary accounting known as the price system was devised in an age of Eurasian feudalism in order to distribute the fruits of industry and conquest in a structured class society—to determine who was to get what of scarce resources. Money worked as an instrument of social control for the master element in the society because the holders of the greatest number of debt certificates could exert a monopoly on stores of goods and resource supplies and thus influence trade practices.

To those who have exercised these privileges by exploiting the pools of petroleum and stores of combustible materials (now including uranium) the prospects of pioneering a new distribution device to make the alternate energy sources available in usable forms seems indeed baffling —not because of the engineering problems involved, but mostly because of this thing called monetary exploitation. It was difficult enough trying to maintain a monopoly over coal and oil reserves when they were in their bonanza era. Uranium ore deposits can be controlled by cartel arrangement. But how do you go about exercising ownership claims on wind, water, sunshine and plant life which garners energy direct from the heavenly orbit itself? To American Indians that would be the supreme sacrilege—to the businessman it is the enigma known as the "energy problem".

Toward a More Sustainable Society

Canada and the United States in recent years have been on an oil consuming binge that has no precedent in human history—and appetites for consumer goods, whetted during that great splurge of affluence, have not abated. However, as the spin-off effects caused by the threat to conventional materials supply, reach to the heart of the money economy, some distressing consequences have become manifest. We seem to be caught up on a treadmill, which demands an ever faster turnover of merchandise in order to yield more man-hours of employment to create more purchasing power to keep the tempo constantly accelerating. And thus, we strive for more "development" toward an unknown destination. Create "jobs" as long as you can stimulate physical "development". Willis Harmer, speaking to the Academy of Science in the U.S., put it this way: "We are exhausting fossil fuels, ruining soil fertility, unbalancing ecosystems and distorting human values and institutions in the greatest energy-spending spree of all time, at the expense of future generations."

As the great search for energy and other materials proceeds, the disruption to the "economy" is reflected in fluctuating interest rates, unpredictable mortgage charges and general bewilderment. The voting public can best register its frustration at the polling booths, so they tend to turf-out any incumbent who fails to deliver instant gratification in the quest for stability. Those administrators taking their turn at the helm, seek to "balance the budget" while those on the outside looking in, can only sit back and demand, "let's get the economy rolling."

But every day it is getting more obvious that what is needed is not an increase in Gross National Product, but a sustainable society based on what the environment can carry without stress. By this criteria, none of the political philosophies dominant at this time are dedicated to this end or planning for it. From left to right, from Communism to Fascism, all are more concerned with power and privilege than organizing to meet the basic needs of people now alive, and conserving for generations yet unborn.

And so, the ideological war continues. When politicians proceed on the assumption that man is separate from nature and its master, then the drive for group privilege, class interest, or individual acquisition of wealth becomes an issue for dispute. Willis Harmer, writing in *The Futurist* remarks that when we begin to see ourselves as "an integral part of the natural world instead of apart from it, then many complex issues will quickly resolve themselves." And again, Lester R. Brown concludes: "Without an environmental ethic that preserves the biological and agronomic underpinnings of society, civilization will collapse."

Time for Some Vision-Seeking

But is this not the same medicine that was prescribed by the wise men of the aboriginal societies? For centuries—no, millenia—before the arrival of Western commercialism, the many societies that made up the North American mosaic had learned to honour the energy of the sun. From the soil of the earth, from the heart of the seed, came a pale, embryonic plant to rise up and drink the energy strength of the sun, and to blossom forth with new life. This was energy flow of a natural order, but again, it was the same. For it, Indians felt humble before the sun.

The sun could give life and it could take life, so it was respected in a hundred different ways.

The solar scientists of the ancient Mayas and Toltecs were instrumental in creating a wonderfully accurate sun calendar, and acquired a knowledge of astronomy, which was unsurpassed elsewhere in the world. The Incas had no word for north and south—only east and west, the rising and setting of the sun. The Pawnee declared that life and death were determined by the sun and, like lovers, provided a male and female, a negative and positive flow of energy. When a child was born to Zuni parents, the infant was lifted up to receive energy and spirit from Father Sun. The Lakota renewed their dedication to life in the Sun Dance.

Tribe after tribe developed their different rituals. But in the last analysis all were the same. To them the sun was the giver of light. The sun was the giver of life. When the people prayed to the sun, they prayed for life. There is nothing superstitious about that behavior—it is scientifically rational.

Centuries before the scholars of Europe discovered that the sun, not man, was the centre of the universe, this was general knowledge among the Indians. Man did not invent light. He was invented by light. He did not create energy. It was here before man. Like the killing of wild game, the important thing is for what purpose that energy is used. Is it used to create shoddy luxury items with built-in obsolescence? Is it used to further the ambitions of ruthless empire builders? Is it to be used as a pawn in the game of prestige posturing?

Western industrial society has conditioned itself to dig around in the bowels of the earth for energy, and to rip the skin off the surface of the earth in search of coal, while we ignore the 47% of the sun's strength, which is readily available. If at this juncture of history, a dead-end seems to be looming the problem is entirely of our own making. There is no "energy crisis" but there is a social crisis in the making as we see the gregarious disciples of "growth" rushing headlong into confrontation with the immutable and sacred laws of the Creator. We should ask ourselves: "Do the balance sheets of "business" adventurism reflect more realism than the system of checks and balances governing the ecological world?" Only human arrogance would suggest such insolence.

It is arrogance that leads us to ignore reality, and it is arrogance that prompts us to conjure up delusions of self-image. We might ask, why have Native People not integrated into the now predominant social pattern of North America? Do Native People, who have only recently been removed from tribal surroundings, possess a lesser propensity for the more complicated involvement of industrial life? For many years the conventional prejudice went something like this: Indians are not like us because they are "savages", lesser creatures on a lower rung of the human ladder; the tribal state is just a part of the gradation in the process of evolution; they do not integrate quickly because they cannot learn to practice our superior ways.

Today this concept is being dismissed as sheer ethnocentric pap. Indians do not integrate chiefly because they cannot countenance what they perceive to be a route to social suicide. To the rapacious world of competitive exploitive enterprise, many feel a sense of concealed spiritual revulsion. They cannot understand why this "price" oriented society can allocate millions of dollars in aid for the poor of foreign lands while they ignore many Native groups who have been pushed almost to the brink of oblivion. In remote areas lack of housing, sanitation, health-care and destruction of animal habitat almost seals their fate. They cannot understand why their "Christian" neighbours do not follow the simple morality of Christ when it comes to "business dealing". This they identify as "the forked tongue" syndrome.

But there are other facets of the question of social organization. Many academics in the field of sociology are today pointing out that societies are simple or complex for the reason that cultures can be simply integrated with fewer elements, or they can be composed of many parts in a complicated fashion. However, the complex societies are not necessarily more advanced than the simple ones.

This being the case, dare we speculate that Western industrial accounting has become so entangled and dominated by financial accounting that it is foundering on elements of its own obscurantism? In the field of finance for example, this is eminently clear for we have now arrived at the state where those professionals known as "economists" are so confused with the ramifications of their own subject matter that their credibility has been lost in a welter of guesses, mumbo-jumbo and opinions. As one wag remarked, "If all the economists were laid end to end, they would not reach a conclusion." The methodology of science, in contrast, still manages to steer a course grounded on fact, so long as scientists can manage to remain uncompromised by the financial embrace. It is a baffling admixture. At this point, both the aboriginal people and large segments of the predominantly "white" society are beginning to show apprehension about their future.

And it is also at this time that we should take note of another interesting phenomenon. Tribal people have always seen a need to congregate for mutual protection because security lies in belonging to something larger than a single individual. These associations have social value, but they carry with them a demand for responsibility. They create their own generalship from within. By nature we are really all tribal creatures because we crave to show that we belong to something greater than ourselves. Most of the treaty Indians in Canada and elsewhere choose even the cramped quarters of reservation life because it affords a bond of mutual affinity. But the socially conscious members of the great racial mosaic known as the "general public", perceiving that all is not well in that melange called the "economy", have also started to form clans for mutual protection. According to the *Journal of Commerce* (October 17, 1978 issue) there are between 10,000 and 15,000 citizen action groups (environment, consumer, neighbourhood, etc.) in the United States alone plus a sizable complement in Canada and Mexico as well.

The motivation of all this inter-tribal loyalty stems from a feeling of rejection. We are rejected when we are denied food; we react when demeaned by a lower standard of living than the average of the tribe; and we are sometimes moved to violence when a neighouring tribe acts to disturb nature's balance and endangers our food supply. And this is just another way of saying that regional disparities breed regional resentments; tax loopholes and tax shelters do not make for intertribal harmony; pollution of water systems that affect wildlife and drinking water are anti-social in the extreme; and the proliferation of nuclear bombs which threaten to exterminate us all, is the crowning affront. The time has come when vision seeking on a major scale must become the order-of-the-day.

The Move to Safer Ground

At the beginning of this treatise, the point was made that the best accommodation that can happen when peoples of differing backgrounds come together, is when the best of ALL CULTURES involved are drawn upon freely and the dross is rejected. As we have observed, the Native People of this continent have made a magnificent contribution to the common good up to this stage in our association. Although it was not within the scope of this study, we have also alluded to some of the more acceptable facets of the imported cultures—their facility for recording data and events in writing, the technique of marshalling information quickly to accomplish a specific goal, the valued research in the fields of medicine and the general methodology of science.

But how about the Indian tradition of sharing with fellow humans within the tribe, within the country, or throughout the continent? Will our vision for tomorrow include the ethic of oneness as related to the environment and all of its living creatures? What are the chances of developing a society wherein the aboriginal people can live, prosper and regain the feeling of pride and self-worth which brought them to so many peaks of accomplishment in the days of their illustrious ancestors?

"There has to be an acceptance of some kind of meaningful relationship with natural things, such as Indians have had," warns the Sioux writer Vine Deloria Jr., "There's got to be an owning up—not just saying that Indians were right and Whites were wrong, but an understanding that the earth, or nature or whatever you want to call it, can't stand the greed and exploitation which are built into Anglo values..."

On the other hand, there has to be an owning up on the part of Indians (and others) that the North America of the year 2,000 is a different world than it was in the year 1400 A.D.; that something has been added—people —millions more people. And that these people now have roots in North American soil and that they will not return willingly to Eurasia, nor will they go there by special request.

As they choose to stay, there is the matter of food, clothing and shelter for over five hundred million people. Where can this be obtained? There is not enough wild plant and animal life growing to meet the need.

Few can realistically think of going back to the days hunting and trapping and gathering wild food for a complete livelihood. An influx of people into the wilderness places for this purpose would be devastating, and the environment (which we are so concerned about preserving) would be the big loser. Like it or not, the entire population of this land-mass called North

America must now devise a new form of environmental husbandry in order to survive and prosper. Together, we must search for a new and modified form of custodianship, an industrial technique which will meet the needs of the entire citizenry, but which meanwhile will assure a balance between cultivated foodstocks, captured solar power and the demographic state of population pressure. The era of hunting and gathering for the majority has become part of history just as surely as the dog-eat-dog concept of European feudalism has become obsolete and inoperative.

It is not the purpose of this book to present a format of how this ecologically balanced state of affairs can be fashioned. But some indication will come from the requirements of the job that needs to be done.

What do we do for example, in tackling the problem of resource depletion as caused by our outmoded concept of compulsive environmental conquest? An antidote for this maleficence can be found in land use planning, materials recycling and repairs to equipment—equipment that has been originally designed and built for durability. Conserve productive land for food cropping, reclaim the reclaimable, and end the era of "planned obsolescence".

The waste of resources must be looked upon as a form of immorality, indeed as an act of criminal practice. When forest areas for example, are clear-cut with little regard to nature's healing power, that is a mental aberration, an unpatriotic act. If this over-cut of forest growth is sold to a foreign nation in the name of "export trade" that is a betrayal of our common interest.

Military involvement abroad and the lucrative arms trade that is associated with it, is another excuse to pillage the resources. It amounts to exporting mayhem at a profit. The nations of the world who have ravaged their own environments to the breaking point are usually the same nations who are either engaged in struggles with other predator societies or are ransacking the more "backward" areas for resources that are perceived to be in short supply on the world market. An example of current interest is the involvement of the major powers in the affairs of the Middle-East, where the timeless quarrels of the desert sheikdoms have taken on a new portent of danger because the major powers prefer to quarrel over purchasing of the desert oil pools rather than exploring the solar option at home.

When we consider the drain on the traditional resource supplies here on the homefront "the day of redress has arrived" as Vine Deloria Jr. the Sioux writer has warned. We are not only undermining the foundations of livelihood for future generations here, but upsetting delicate political equilibriums abroad. Wasteful land-use practices, destruction of wildlife, planned obsolescence, duplication of effort and military involvements are all leading us to rendezvous with destiny. And in this rush toward the "evil day" we all try to rationalize causes. Why not blame it all on technology? Because we see the march of mammoth machines taking their toll, must we assume that we have put our finger on the culprit?

In early chapters, we have noted with admiration how the Indian societies developed such technologies as the canoe, the toboggan, fish-weirs, sun calendars, etc. Yet when we look at today's assault on nature's storehouse, many Indians and some over-sensitive whites, will point to "technology" per se as the great villain in the debauch. It is like saying that traps as used in obtaining furs are the cause of animal extinction; that brothels are built by carpenters' tools therefore hammers and saws are the cause of prostitution.

The important point we must all learn is that man must determine the best use and purpose for this technology and apply it in such a way that does not offend or contravene the laws of nature. If we are going to attain the objective of providing food, clothing and housing for the millions of residents by the new form of "modified industrial custodianship" just referred to, we must learn to be more selective in the technologies we bring into use when dealing with the environment. That specifically, is why the choice of the solar option in harnessing an energy supply must take precedence over such obviously destructive methods as fossil fuels and nuclear power.

In the past, empire builders have been hung up on bigness, centralization and monopolistic ownership control devices. This fixation can be seen in the love for big machinery, mammoth-sized earth-moving projects, and in the building of those huge man-swarms we call cities, now growing into metropolitan megalopoli. But big machinery, we are starting to learn is not necessarily more efficient machinery.

There is a physical relationship in all mechanical equipment that is well known to engineers. It says that the more efficiently machines are made to operate, the more they tend to scale down in size. This principle can be noted in such items of technology as watches, radios and household electrical equipment. We can also observe this tendency in the transformation of the family automobile as the big lumbering gas-guzzling chromed-up monsters fade away and the fleets of compact energy-efficient cars take to the highways. On the current scene, another great harbinger of change looms on the horizon in the form of the tiny silicone flake—a complex of electrical switches controlling currents that activate the array of computers, calculators and robots that are taking over the work of ponderous equipment and reducing the work-load on people too. This is scientific efficiency.

But it would appear that there are two forces working at cross-purposes even in the field of technology, or is it human interference in the choice of application? Only in the world of mega-projects, where the assault on the environment is the greatest—earth moving, mining and smelting, timber devastation etc.—are the mechanical juggernauts getting bigger. In contrast the assembly plants, factories and processing establishments are changing gears to increased efficiency per unit of output at diminished energy expenditure. In the latter case we are provided with yet another opportunity to conserve through recycling. If much of the old and obsolete plants and equipment is now to be scrapped in favour of the new technology, can the metals not be melted down, making much of the frontier mining for new ore unnecessary? Of course it can. That too, is progress.

Conservation of resources also means that human habitations should be located away from present congested cities and upon soil that is unsuitable for growing food crops, yet close enough to specific industries so that excess energy is not used for transportation.

From the foregoing, it would appear that some major adjustments in living patterns are not only advisable but are inevitable. The times demand new and more appropriate technologies and those who are out-of-step with the realities of the day will be swept along on the tide of social necessity, and a growing avalanche of public opinion. King Canute could not hold back the incoming tide, and neither can financial jugglers successfully challenge the laws of thermo-dynamics which were laid down as the instructions of The Creator. Most tribal people can understand that credo. Lester R. Brown, of Worldwatch Institute (a non-profit research group founded by private foundations and United Nations agencies) points to the public interest groups throughout the country as "the engines that are powering the transition."

The new appropriate technologies of tomorrow, powered by both direct and indirect solar energy, are quite capable of providing the entire population of this continent with all of the necessities of life when efficiently oriented. And they can do this with a diminishing number of man-hours expended in human toil if duplication of effort is minimized, export of raw materials markedly curtailed and a full load-factor maintained on the new modified technology. This makes it important that the Native People be involved, not only in the process of production, but sharing equitably in the fruits of such participation. It means that education for such enterprises should be freely available and that consultation with Native People be a prerequisite to all social development which affects their well-being. And it means that many of our cherished notions of dog-eat-dog economic competition must be subordinated to a new ethic of sharing.

A Light on the Horizon

When we say that adjustments are not only advisable but inevitable, it is encouraging to look at the transition or mental adjustments, that are taking place even now before our very eyes. A degree of gathering awareness is discernible throughout our society.

Magazines and periodicals are popularizing the merits of rural life, explaining methods of soil improvement, introducing the design and construction of ingenious solar applications and explaining the merits of living with nature. What's more, they are being avidly read by an increasing list of subscribers. Television programmers have discovered that there is a deep hunger for more knowledge of the wilderness to the extent that nature and wildlife shows have captured "prime-time" ratings on many stations. Expeditions into out-of-the-way places with improved photographic equipment have reached a new plateau of interest. These are all symptoms of a new evolving awareness.

But that is not all. It speaks of a new stewardship, a nurturing attitude toward both wild and domesticated creatures, a new appreciation of Mother Earth and of all sustenance she is able to provide, and a rejoicing in the pleasures that this intimacy can bring. It speaks of a new tranquility that can flow from the application of a technology that is made subservient, for the purpose of creating leisure and comfort. And it dreams of an enriched spiritual fulfillment that is released when ethnic bridges are easily traversed and leisure time can be directed into such cultural pursuits as drama, music, art, literature and pageantry. Does this sound like the kind of world where Indians can mingle with Whites on an even footing and enjoy the feeling of belonging? At least, it is a goal toward which we can all aspire.

The North American Indians of yesterday lived in their world as ecological participants rather than commercial competitors. During centuries of residency, spanning eons of time, they have wandered the length and breadth of this vast and magnificent continent and have demonstrated an ability to adapt to changes when circumstances in the natural world have altered. With the "Johnny-come-lately" cousins, who have arrived within the short interval of four hundred years or so, they have shared both their territory and their cultural attainments without stint. Today, we all stand at a new cross-roads that demands a change in direction, an adjustment in outlook that will bring about some form of ecological balance to assure our continued survival as a human species.

The North American Indians now entering the twenty-first century, are intellectually capable of adjusting to new techniques of survival and they have a vision of what might lie ahead. In the present, they find themselves trapped into a rear-guard battle to retain the limited land holdings and aboriginal rights that were guaranteed to them. In order to share in the bounty of their own homeland, they often find themselves cajoled into joining a game of economic poker which offers only wages for short term benefit, but waste, pollution, poverty and war as a final prize.

We are All at the cross-roads.

We all need the vision experience.

102

VISION FOR MY PEOPLE

Grandfather, Great Spirit,
Today I sat for a short while in the thundering silence of your solitude.
And as I sat there I saw a vision of how it was and how it is
And how it was supposed to be, here in this part of your creation.
I thought about, and I saw with my limited vision,
The power and the sacredness and the beauty of your creation.
I give thanks for this new day.
Kitchi meegwetch!

This morning that strong warrior, our elder brother Sun
Came up over the mountain, and he looked into my eyes, and he said,
The time for sleep is over now. You must get up and work.
I have brought a new day and a new chance—maybe a new way
To see things. You must get up and do your part
To make this a new world.

I looked and I saw the vision of how it was
When I was still a little boy.
The birds were singing their songs and building their nests
In the way they were taught so long ago.
The animals and the fishes and the plants and the sky world,
They went about their work in the way they too were told so long ago.

I looked again and I saw how it was supposed to be.
I listened and I heard it said that all things in your creation
Had been created—male and female
And of every kind, the fishes and the birds and the ones that walk and crawl
And the ones that grow with roots in the ground,
Each had been given its original instructions.
All had been told that they were to grow to their greatest beauty
And reproduce themselves
And return again to the earth mother.
In that way your creation would be on-going, forever fresh and new,
Forever power, and beauty, and sacredness.

Then I looked at the vision of how it is and I saw this,—
I saw might and destitution.
I saw prisons and vengeance.
I saw a vision of the greatest desecration in the history of man.
I saw leaders who are fools but who believed they were gods in their own right
I saw those who were leading everything, even our earth mother,
Into a final and total annihilation, without reprieve.
And I saw that you will not let it be that way,
Grandfather.

I looked beyond the monstrous stupidity of these leaders
And I saw hope.
For you had raised up good people who saw the final death.
And they said, No! you cannot go that way!
For we have reached out our hearts and our minds and our hands
Across the continents and the oceans of the world.
And we will surround you and circumscribe you
With an unbroken and unbreakable ring of prayer and hope
For the continuation of our children and our future.
That is how it has to be.

Art Solomon
Ojibway Spiritual Advisor

WE ALL FACE THIS CHALLENGE TOGETHER
Robert Obonsawin

We live in a society that sees the environment as a tool to be exploited in order that those who control the economic system continue to prosper. We call that PROGRESS.

We live in a society that utilizes its standard of living to create false material needs. We call that INITIATIVE.

We live in a society that encourages competition, so that only the strongest survive. We call that FAIR PLAY.

Traditional Native societies are the complete opposite. Nature must be protected so that it will benefit the next generations. Sharing ensures the survival and well-being of all people. The individual is respected as a unique human being, able to function within the community.

We face a society intent on exhausting non-renewable resources.

We face a society intent on destroying itself with its technology.

We face a society intent on establishing a "two founding nations" theory with a total disregard for the values, traditions, and life styles of Canada's original inhabitants.

ALL CANADIANS FACE THESE PROBLEMS AND ALL CANADIANS MUST ADDRESS THEMSELVES TO RESOLVING THESE CONFLICTS IF WE ARE TO SURVIVE.

BIBLIOGRAPHY

I
CHAPTER

Name Calling Made Popular

In 1929, the noted linguist Edward Sapir, arranged the multipicity of
Native languages and dialects of North America (some sources estimate
over 600 in all) into six major stocks of derivation, using a method called
glottochronology. This system of grouping makes the study of Native
languages much simpler and indeed, it is a great help in tracing early migra-
tions. However, it would still be an immense task to sort out all the words
and names that have filtered into the lexicon of the three main recipients
English, French and Spanish.

> *Indians of the United States:* Clark Wissler (Doubleday 1940,
> 1966)

This is an excellent book of reference because, in his treatment of the sub-
ject, the author centres his discourse around the six major linguistic stocks.
On page 330, he also gives a small sampling of words and names from the
United States' scene.

In Canada, a fairly comprehensive selection can be made from books
such as:

> *The Origin and Meaning of Place Names in Canada:* G.H.
> Armstrong (MacMillan, 1972)
> *The MacMillan Book of Canadian Place Names:* William B.
> Hamilton (MacMillan, 1983)
> *Selected Bibliography of Canadian Toponomy:* Department
> of Mines and Surveys, 1964

A dictionary such as Webster's New World College Edition, serves a purpose in a quest for words and their tribal origins. The word "coyote" we can
read, comes from the Nahuatl language spoken by the Aztecs. This small
brush wolf was named after a thorny bush found in Mexico and called
"coyotillo" plant by the same Aztecs. In this way, a substantial list of words
can be compiled.

2

CHAPTER

The Gift of Survival

The Canadian Indian: Fraser Symington (McClelland Stewart, 1969)

This book dealing with the northern sector of the North American Continent, presents with no less than 282 illustrations, the various ways and devices used by the more than 50 tribal groups of this area to adapt to their particular environment. The tools they used, the modes of transportation and types of housing used are described with unusual understanding. What we have to realize most specifically here is that these were the tools and inventions that made the survival of the first arrivals from Europe possible—these and the help and hospitality that went with them.

The Daily Life of the Aztecs: Jacques Soustelle (Pelican, 1961)

As we know, the Aztecs fell heir to the craftmanship of the Toltecs. These attainments are discussed in some detail in this book. Special attention is directed to Page 231.

Indians of the United States: Clark Wissler (Doubleday, 1966)

The contents of this book is organized in such a way as to assemble linguistic families from various parts of the continent for study. The various methods of adaptation are outlined and notation made of the interactions with people of the Western culture upon first contact. The entire book is a treasure of information. Chapter 19 deals with the subject of acculturation in its reverse aspects—when many of the newcomers attempted to immerse themselves in the cultures of the Native societies.

3
CHAPTER

The True Meaning of Sport

The Rise and Fall of Maya Civilization: J. Eric Thompson
(Univ. of Oklahoma, 1964)

The intellectual and artistic achievements of the Classic Maya period were immense. Much of the success must be attributed to the creation and maintenance of group spirit. This was largely attained through the fostering of group sports. See Chapter 4 for an understanding of how this concept of community action was diffused throughout the society and what it accomplished.

Red Man's America: Ruth M. Underhill (University of Chicago, 1971)

This book contains a multitude of references to games and athletics. They include: archery, ball race, cup and pin, dice, racing, football, kick ball, lacrosse, horse racing, quoits, ring-and-pin, shinny, shuffleboard, snow snake, stick-ball, tops, tug-of-war, wrestling.

First Among the Hurons: Max Gros-Louis (Harvest House, 1973)

This book contains sections (Pages 23-39) wherein the author discusses the difference in attitude toward hunting practices from experiences gained in the Quebec woods, as a guide to white hunters. Chief Gros-Louis finds it difficult to credit some of these practices as civilized.

The Canadian Indian: Fraser Symington

For an example of overkill in its most extreme form, Chapter 18 (Page 217) is topical. This chapter is entitled, "The Great Buffalo Kill". Author Symington deals with the who and why of this slaughter.

Custer Died for Your Sins: Vine Deloria Jr. (MacMillan, 1969)

On Pages 23 and 41 the author, a Lakota Indian, deals with the different attitudes that still prevail toward fishing and what goes on in the wilderness places.

4
CHAPTER

The Gift of Better Health

Information contained in this chapter was gleaned from many sources, including personal interviews. Four source books are easily available.

Earth Medicine: Earth Food: Weiner (Macmillan, 1972)
Indian Herbology of North America: Hutches (Homeopathy Press)
A Treasure of Indian Herbs: Scully (Crown)
American Indian Medicine: Virgil J. Vogel (University of Oklahoma Press, 1970)

The above-listed publications are good in themselves, but possibly the most complete compendium of Indian medical knowledge is contained in the 584 page book entitled, "American Indian Medicine", and first published in 1970.

This book is of outstanding reference value because of two factors: (i) It is continental in it's scope; (ii) Chapters are arranged in such a way that quick reference is possible. For example, Chapter 7 deals with Indian Therapeutic Methods under such sub-headings as: Drugs; Drugless Therapy; Treatment of Internal Ailments; Treatment of Injuries; Obstetrics; Gynecology; Dentistry; Diet and Hygiene.

A suggested procedure, if one wishes to glean the greatest bounty of information, is to use this as a pivotal reference and cross-refer to the other sources.

First Among the Hurons: Max Gros-Louis

Treatment of the common cold and use of Vitamin C is dealt with on Page 117.

Many Mexicos: Lesley Byrd Simpson (Univ. of California, 1969)

See Page 111 for reference to the Code of Burgos.

5

CHAPTER

The Gift of Agriculture and Food

Americas First Civilization: Michael D. Coe
(McClelland, 1968)

Special attention is drawn to Chapter 2 entitled, "Nomads Become Settled Farmers" (Page 25). Here the author discusses at some length how, in recent times, archaeologist MacNeish, and botanist Mandelsdorf, teamed up to explore the development of corn from its ancestral stocks. This was accomplished by the Olmec Indians sometime about 5000-3500 B.C. The author gives us an excellent summation written in easily understood terminology. The remainder of the book is a treasure trove of information concerning other phases of the Olmec culture.

The Daily Life of the Aztecs: Jacques Souselle

The marketplace is a good locale to study the extent of agricultural attainments of any society. In this book (Pages 36 to 48) the author lists the bountiful display as seen by the early Spaniards visiting Tenochtitlan, the Aztec Capital.

Indians of the Americas: John Collier (W.W. Norton and Co. Ltd., 1947)

A partial list of Indian field crops appears on Page 33. A description of chinampas or floating gardens as used by the Aztecs is to be found on Page 81. On Page 32, the number of wild growths cultivated for use by Indians and now utilized by the world, aggregates more than half of the present agricultural wealth. Estimates by some writers and authorities run even higher.

The Trail of the Iroquois: G. Elmore Reaman (Peter Martin, 1967)

It is a well known fact that the Iroquois were the leading agriculturists of the northern regions. On Pages 19 and 20, author Reaman gives us an outline of the extent of cultivation that took place in the Finger Lakes area.

6
CHAPTER

The Influences of Folk Democracy

The American Heritage Book of Indians: Wm. Brandon (Dell, 1961)

Europeans arriving in North America in the days of conquest found forms of social administration so different from their own, that it often had ideological repercussions in the home establishment back in Europe. Some of these are dealt with on Pages 136 to 251.

The Social Organization of the Aztecs

To gain an insight into Aztec governing methods in synoptic form, a reading of Chapter 4 from, "The Indians of the Americas" by John Collier is helpful.

For a more in-depth reading see, "The Daily Life of the Aztecs", by Jacquest Soustelle, a noted French ethnologist who writes from a viewpoint of cultural detachment. On Page 231, he writes: "The ancient Mexicans loved their books, and when the fanatical hands of Zumarraga hurled thousands upon thousands of these precious manuscripts into the fire, the flames destroyed a very great part of their culture." Soustelle expresses his outrage, but continues to pick up as many pieces as he can find from the debris.

The League of the Iroquois

Resource/Reading List (Canadian Association in Support of the Native Peoples, 16 Spadina Rd., Toronto M5R 2S7; 1982, and supplement), good listing of books on the Iroquois.

The League of the Iroquois: Lewis H. Morgan (republished by World Publishing Co., 1963)

One of the earliest studies was an essay under this same title by Lewis H. Morgan in 1904. This is now difficult to obtain. However, see the following sources for quick reference.

American Heritage Book of Indians Wm. Brandon (See Pages 174-178)

Indians of the Americans John Collier (See Pages 200-204)

The Trail of the Iroquois Indians G. Elmore Reaman (See Pages 25-29)

Red Man's America Ruth M. Underhill (See Pages 84-109)

The Pueblo Cultures of New Mexico

American Heritage Book of Indians (See Pages 108-123)

The Muskhogean Societies

Indians of the United States Wissler (See Pages 160-165)

The American Heritage Book of Indians Wm. Brandon (See Pages 138-147)

The Pawhaton Confederacy

The American Heritage Book of Indians Brandon (See Pages 154-159)

7
CHAPTER

A Vision Experience for Tomorrow

Indians of the United States Carl Wissler
Indians showed a sensitivity toward their environment which the Western mind seems to have almost lost. Wissler devotes Chapter 21 to discovering the Mystery of the Indian Mind. See Page 298.

America's First Civilization Michael D. Coe
Chapter 7 of this book discusses the religious orientation that took place when the Olmecs (first agriculturists of North America) became settled farmers—how the Rain God and God of Springtime fostered fertility and the passing of the omnipotent sun across the heavens provided the food crops and the cycles of time that could be measured. This, of course, became the origin and the underpinning of methodical studies, astronomical knowledge and the forms of sun worship that permeated Meso-america. This is noted particularly in the Classic Period of the Maya civilization which rose to such heights of cultural excellence at a time roughly parallel to the time of Christ.

God is Red Vine Deloria Jr. (Grosset Dunlop, 1973)
This author is a Lakota Sioux, who studied Christian theology with a view to becoming a minister or priest, but changed back to his ancestral form of worship. He perceived in the Christian religion an estrangement from nature which he could not reconcile within himself. In the commercialism of the Western world, he sees still more complete degradation of his traditional values. This articulate author is also interviewed in Vol. 5, No. 1 issue of the Indian periodical, "Akwesasne Notes".

Solar Energy—The Indian Way

This article, by Tom Barry, first appeared in the publication "Native Self-Sufficiency" (October, 1979). It was written for Akwesasne Notes Vol. 1, No. 3. The same issue carried articles vehemently opposed to nuclear power development.

Building a Sustainable Society Lester R. Brown (Norton, 1981)

This author heads a Washington based organization called Worldwatch Institute, which concerns itself with matters pertaining to the checks and balances between world resource supplies and global population growth.

Part 1, entitled, "Converging Demands", may be summarized in this one quotation: "One problem with the free market is that it is no respecter of carrying capacity. Market forces can destroy fisheries, forests, grasslands, and croplands. The market has no alarm that sounds when the carrying capacity of the biological system has been transgressed." About 300 pages of proof is then presented to show that this carrying capacity is now under great stress, if not overtaxed. This is a new addition to many such books now starting to appear on the shelves of North American libraries.